# Clearly, I Didn't Think This Through

# Clearly, I Didn't Think This Through

## The Story of One Tall Girl's Impulsive, Ill-Conceived, and Borderline Irresponsible Life Decisions

ANNA GOLDFARB

BERKLEY BOOKS, NEW YORK

**THE BERKLEY PUBLISHING GROUP**
**Published by the Penguin Group**
**Penguin Group (USA) Inc.**
**375 Hudson Street, New York, New York 10014, USA**

Penguin Group (Canada), 90 Eglinton Avenue East, Suite 700, Toronto, Ontario M4P 2Y3, Canada (a division of Pearson Penguin Canada Inc.) • Penguin Books Ltd., 80 Strand, London WC2R 0RL, England • Penguin Ireland, 25 St. Stephen's Green, Dublin 2, Ireland (a division of Penguin Books Ltd.) • Penguin Group (Australia), 707 Collins Street, Melbourne, Victoria 3008, Australia (a division of Pearson Australia Group Pty. Ltd.) • Penguin Books India Pvt. Ltd., 11 Community Centre, Panchsheel Park, New Delhi—110 017, India • Penguin Group (NZ), 67 Apollo Drive, Rosedale, Auckland 0632, New Zealand (a division of Pearson New Zealand Ltd.) • Penguin Books, Rosebank Office Park, 181 Jan Smuts Avenue, Parktown North 2193, South Africa • Penguin China, 87 Jaiming Center, 27 East Third Ring Road North, Chaoyang District, Beijing 100020, China

Penguin Books Ltd., Registered Offices: 80 Strand, London WC2R 0RL, England

This book is an original publication of The Berkley Publishing Group.


Interior text design by Laura K. Corless.



PUBLISHING HISTORY
Berkley trade paperback edition / November 2012

Library of Congress Cataloging-in-Publication Data

Goldfarb, Anna.
Clearly, I didn't think this through : the story of one tall girl's impulsive, ill-conceived, and borderline irresponsible life decisions / Anna Goldfarb. — Berkley trade paperback ed.
p. cm.
ISBN 978-0-425-24532-3
1. Goldfarb, Anna. 2. Self-realization in women. I. Title.
PS3607.o4536c57 2012
814'.6—dc23
[B] 2012029462

PRINTED IN THE UNITED STATES OF AMERICA

10 9 8 7 6 5 4 3 2 1

*Penguin is committed to publishing works of quality and integrity.
In that spirit, we are proud to offer this book to our readers;
however, the story, the experiences, and the words are the author's alone.*

To my parents, for not charging me rent.

Yet.

# CONTENTS

# CHAPTER 1

# Future Plans

"Well, look who decided to show up." My mom turned around to face me and put her hands on her hips, balancing the cordless phone on her shoulder. "It's okay, Officer. She's here. In fact, she just walked through the door. Thanks for your help. Yeah, we've got it from here."

My name is Anna Goldfarb. I'm a 6'1", barely employed, single, thirty-three-year-old Jewish woman. And, judging by the look on my mother's face, I was in trouble.

"Hey, guys." I gave a faint smile. "Who were you just talking to on the phone?" Looking around the kitchen, I saw my mom, my younger sister, Rachel, and her dog, Ginger, all glaring at me. My dad was at the dining room table, clicking around on his ancient Toshiba laptop. The keys stick, which makes it sound like a leprechaun is doing a tap dance routine when he types an e-mail. No one said anything; my mother tapped her foot.

"What's up? Why is everyone looking at me like I just committed a crime or something?"

"I will have you know that I was just on the phone with the police," my mom said sternly.

"The police? Why? Is everything okay?" The dog growled at me when I reached over to pet her head. She always does that.

"Well, when we didn't hear from you and I saw that you didn't come home last night, I had no idea what to think!"

"Wait, you called *the police* because I didn't come home last night? Really? Is this a joke? Oh my God, Mom, I'm *fine*."

"I tried to call your cell phone at least a dozen times, but you didn't pick up, Anna. Didn't you get my messages?"

"I tried to call you, too," Rachel said, clutching her dog. "No one knew where you were. We've been freaking out, like, all morning."

"Your father was worried out of his mind!" My mom gestured toward my dad. His huge glasses reflected the computer screen. He seemed calm. "Weren't you, Roy?" my mom prodded. "Weren't you worried?"

"What? Oh, yes, yes," he mumbled. "Very worried. Very." Then he went back to staring at the computer.

"I'm sorry, guys. I didn't get any of your messages. Hold on, let me check my phone." It took a while to find it because it was buried under a few things, but sure enough, there were seventeen missed calls. Scrolling through, it became clear that everyone on the planet had been trying to reach me today.

"Why didn't you pick up your phone?" my mom shrieked.

"It must've been on vibrate or something! I'm sorry." I put the phone to my ear and heard the first message, left around seven A.M. It was my mother, slightly agitated.

"Hey, Anna. I saw that you didn't come home last night. Your car's not here and you're not in your bed. I want to make sure that you're okay. Give me a call when you get this." I deleted it, and then listened to the next one in the queue, which was also from my mother.

"Hey, Anna. It's eight A.M. I still haven't heard from you. Give me a call." After that, the messages increased with alarm. My mom's voice changed from concern to straight-up panic.

By the seventh message, anxiety had firmly taken over. "Anna, I'm really starting to worry here. It's almost nine thirty A.M. and we haven't heard anything from you. Please call home when you get this."

Rachel got in on the manhunt around then, leaving a few panicked messages of her own. "Anna, call home. Mom is worried."

My best friend, Kat, even left one around ten A.M. "Yo, your mom just called me looking for you. I told her I had no clue where you were. Did you stay over at Alvin's last night or something? I hope you just got some action and aren't dead. Anyway, call home and talk to your mom. And, if you got action, call me later and tell me how it went. Bye."

The last message on the voice mail is where shit got crazy. My mother's voice was wobbly. "Anna, we've contacted the police. We have no idea where you are. Please, please call us when you get this message. Oh, God!"

Apparently my impromptu slumber party had left me one step away from having my picture plastered on the side of a milk carton. I could see it now:

*Name: Anna Goldfarb*

*Height: 6'1"*
*Hair: Brown*
*Eyes: Green*

*Weight: Curvy (Even in a police description, I'm sure my family wouldn't print my actual weight, but instead opt for a vague estimation to spare me the humiliation.)*

*Last seen wearing: A black hooded sweatshirt and black jeans.*

*Age: 33*

*She likes Black Sabbath, Mexican food, reality television, and the first two movies in the* Back to the Future *trilogy. If found, please contact the police.*

"Well, the good news is that I'm not dead, so you can call off the search."

"I was this close to calling the hospitals, young lady," my mother said. Her fingers were spaced roughly a millimeter apart.

"Mom, I stayed over at a friend's house. Don't worry about it. Oh my God, I never stay over at anyone's house and the one night I do, you all panic. It's not a big deal."

You could tell I hadn't planned to spend the night because my eye makeup from last night was smeared and trace amounts of dog drool were crusted in my hair. Don't ask.

"Why didn't you pick up when I called?" she demanded. "I was freaking out!"

"Clearly, you're still freaking out. I got that. My phone was in my purse, which was in his closet. I mean, the closet." Oh shit. My cover was blown.

"*His* closet? Which friend was this exactly?"

"Look, Mom, don't worry about it. I'm fine. I'm alive. There's no need for law enforcement to intervene." I had finally hooked up with a guy and my mother had called the police; you know, totally normal things to happen to a thirty-three-year-old woman, right?

The dog barked at me like she wanted some answers about who this guy was, too.

"Shut up, Ginger," I moaned.

Rachel crinkled her nose at me. "Hey, don't tell my dog to shut up."

"Well, don't have a shitty dog then."

At that moment, all I wanted to do was kick off my boots and have a long, hot shower. I wanted to wash away the events from the night before. Mostly I wanted to wash off my mascara, which was flaking off like it'd had enough of being yelled at, too. I dreamed about the second I could slip into a comfy pair of sweatpants. I had been fantasizing about wearing them for the past two hours since I'd woken up in Alvin's bed. That's the thing about wearing tight jeans; it makes wearing anything with an elastic waistband feel like a hug from an angel.

Truthfully, I was too hungover to have a conversation with anyone about anything. Taking off my sunglasses to meet their gaze felt like an unreasonable request, like caring about Lindsay Lohan's prison record or getting in an argument with a third-grader about Pokémon.

My dad finally looked up from his computer. "And when exactly are you leaving?" He wasn't talking about me leaving to go back home. I was home. Or rather, I was in their home, having moved back into my parents' house about a year before. He was really asking when I planned on getting my life together. And it's not that I didn't agree with him, it's just that I didn't feel quite ready to give up my life of leisure, at least not yet.

It's not like I didn't watch my high school and college friends fall into line, one by one. As they became more stable, settling into lives that seemed plucked from the pages of an IKEA catalog, I strangely found myself regressing, exploring things that most people got out of their system when they graduated high school. As my friends hung works of art in their freshly painted foyers, I tacked up Michael J. Fox posters on my bedroom wall. As they set up savings accounts and monthly budgets in Excel spreadsheets, I dipped into my paltry funds for beer money. We looked at each other like we were different species and in a way we were: They were *Homo sapiens maturus* and I was *Homo sapiens immaturus*. If we mated, we'd probably start a whole new breed of human being.

Frankly, despite my best efforts, I just wasn't well versed in how to be an adult. There were entire swaths of skill sets that I wasn't fluent in. Maturity used to be something I aspired to, but as a woman in my thirties, I wear it like an ill-fitting sweater that I've flung into the corner, hoping one day that I would pick it up and it would magically fit better.

I'm sure my parents wished that they could send me to Adult School to enroll in the following classes:

—*Maintaining a Healthy Relationship 101*
—*Bedroom Decor: Put Some Effort into This, for the Love of God*
—*Wearing Pigtails Is No Longer Cute at Your Age*
—*How to Sleep Like a Human Being and Not Like a Nocturnal Animal*
—*Picking a Viable Career with Reasonable Job Security: A Roundtable Seminar*

And it's not like I didn't want to join my friends on the quest to maturity, but like a cosmic game of duck-duck-goose, the desire just hadn't tapped me on the noggin. I was still sitting cross-legged on the carpet, watching everyone around me get the head tap, scramble to their feet, and run around in circles. Life hadn't goosed me yet; at least that was what I told myself.

And believe me, no one was more surprised than I was to find myself in this position of needing lessons in maturity. I grew up by the book, doing everything right. I studied hard in school; I spent my early twenties striving to build a career for myself. But by following the rules, I'd missed out on a lot of things, like staying over at a guy's house on a whim.

"So, you lose your minds when I'm not here and now you're asking when I'll be gone again. Unbelievable." I rolled my eyes.

"Your mother and I are concerned, that's all," he said calmly.

"Okay. What exactly are you guys concerned about?"

They exchanged looks, and my mom nodded for him to keep going. "Where do I start? What are your future plans? You have no job and no money. When are you going to get your life back on track?"

"Dad—" I started to defend myself, but he interrupted me.

"It's a fair question, right? You've been living here for over a year. Maybe it's time for the bird to leave the nest. Again." He made a little shooing motion to hammer the point home.

"I think it's great that Anna's home again, recharging her batteries, saving some money, paying down her bills. A lot of people are doing that these days. It's pretty common." I looked around the kitchen in the direction of the voice and saw my older sister, Sarah, on my mom's computer monitor, offering her two cents via Skype.

"Hey, Sarah. You're in on this, too?"

"I told Mom that you probably weren't dead. Glad to see I was right. Oh, and Julianna says hi. Say hi, Julianna!" She picked up my niece and placed her on her knee. The baby waved into the camera, gurgling and cooing.

"Hi, sweetie! Auntie isn't dead. But everyone's decided to have a life intervention while I'm tired and hungover, all because I got a little action with this hot, short guy and—"

Sarah covered her baby's ears. "My daughter isn't ready to hear about hangovers and action yet. Let's just keep the conversation about puppies and rainbows, okay?"

My mother piped up. "What your father is trying to say is that we think you should give some thought to your future, that's all."

"You guys want to do this now? Can't I get a shower first?"

"Well, you can't stay here forever, kiddo," he said. "You are an adult. We get that. We do. All we're saying is that maybe you should start looking into your options. We don't want you to be a slacker all day, watching life pass you by."

"Dad, no one's used the word *slacker* since the nineties. You're like two decades late on that. Besides, I'm not slacking around during the day. I'm working on my blog. You know that."

"And how much money have you made on this, uh, *blog* of yours?" He said it like he'd never heard the word before.

"Technically, none. But it has potential! I'm riding the wave. I'm hanging in there, like that little cat on that poster people put in their cubicles. I'm that cat, hanging on the branch with my feet dangling, toughing it out." I raised my hands like I was hanging on to an invisible branch. "You know, hanging in there." The baby laughed when I did that.

My mother cleared her throat before she chimed in. "Honey, you're very talented. We all know that. We love having you here. We love how you cook dinner and help with the food shopping. Your father just wants to know that you have some"—she searched for the right word—"direction."

"I have plenty of direction," I protested. "What can I say? I'm trying my best. It's hard out there with the economy what it is. No one is hiring. No one. I've looked. Believe me, I've looked."

"Have you thought about temping again?" my father suggested, as if he were suddenly channeling a high school guidance counselor.

"Dad, we've gone over this a million times: Temping kills my soul. I'm terrible in offices. I'm not cut out for them. For one thing, I hate office casual clothes. I look like an asshole in khakis. Everyone knows that." Sarah scowled at me over the monitor for swearing. "Oh, sorry, baby. I mean, I look like a dork in khakis. I hate getting up early. And really, humans weren't made to spend their lives in a windowless office, toiling away on a computer. It's not natural."

"You're on your computer all day! That's all you do!" Mom pointed out.

"Yeah, but I'm working on my own projects, not a mindless, pointless exercise for some middle manager somewhere. It's different. Is this what you want for your daughter? To be unhappy?"

"Have you thought about taking a job at the post office? Supposedly, they have excellent benefits."

"Dad, I'm not going to work at the post office. That's probably the dumbest thing I've heard all day. For one thing, I don't like wearing shorts. I hate getting paper cuts. And you know that I burn easily in the sun. I'll figure something out soon, I promise."

"We put you through Barnard for this?" he grumbled, turning his attention back to his laptop. He likes to toss this out from time to time, just to remind me that I'm not living up to my potential.

"I'm just worried that you won't meet someone nice the longer you put this off," my mother said, wringing her hands.

"Mom, I meet plenty of guys. I'm not worried about that."

"What kind of guys are you meeting, Anna? Jewish ones? With nice jobs?"

"Okay, Mom. You got me: I go out with Satan-worshipping homeless orphans. What do you think? I meet normal guys with normal jobs. Once again, don't worry about it. "

"Yes, but do they all have to be *so short*?" She said it like an accusation, like I only date short guys to piss her off.

"Mom! We've been over this a million times, too: I like short guys. No, wait. I love short guys. I always have and I always will. If I were marching in a parade, I'd shout: 'I'm here, I'm into short guys, get used to it.' Why is everyone picking on me today?

I'm not such a terrible person. I mean, it could be worse. I could have a heroin addiction or be pregnant and not know who the father is."

"Why would that even be an issue?" Rachel asked.

"I don't know. I've been watching a lot of *The Maury Povich Show* lately. Honestly, everyone, things aren't so bad in the scheme of things. Can we take a second and get some perspective on this?"

"Why don't you try online dating, like your sister Sarah? It worked for her." My mom thought online dating was the answer to everything. She had never done it, which is probably why she was so enthusiastic about it. One hour wading around on OkCupid would've changed her tune on that. Between the freaks and geeks, it was a war zone in there.

"Everyone, we've been through this, too. I'm terrible at online dating. I have enough anxiety trying to date guys I see in person; I don't need to add stressful, boring coffee dates to the mix. I don't even want a boyfriend right now. Besides, you need money to date, and until my blog takes off, well, let's just say that I'm watching what I spend."

"You mean you're watching what *we* spend," Dad joked.

"Well, you guys are doing great work supporting both the local Philadelphia breweries and several South Philly Mexican restaurants through me. I'm sure that they appreciate your business. Is there anything else about my lifestyle you'd like to attack? We haven't even talked about the fact that I still sleep with a stuffed animal. Wanna call the cops about that, too?"

My father closed his eyes and massaged his temples. My mom sighed heavily.

"Listen, everyone, I hear what you're saying. I don't have my shit together yet. I have no job, no boyfriend, and no plans. If there's nothing else to add, then I'm going to go upstairs to take a shower and wash this dog drool out of my hair because it's crusty and it's grossing me out. So, are we good here?"

My parents both nodded and reluctantly murmured yes. The dog barked because she always barks. The baby gurgled because she doesn't really know how to talk yet. My father went back to ignoring the situation and concentrating on his bulky computer with the sticky keys.

"Guys, don't look at it like you have a thirty-three-year-old living with you. Just pretend that you've gained two sixteen-and-a-half-year-olds." Mom laughed at that.

"From now on, will you just let us know if you're not coming home? Shoot over a text or something," she said.

"All right. Deal. Now, what's for lunch because I'm starving."

# CHAPTER 2

## Your Place or Your Place?

This all started because last night, my friend Alvin invited me over to his house to play board games. The text he shot over read:

> You + me + other people + beers + board games = fun. 7 pm Friday night at my house. You in?

I waited two seconds before I replied:

> Hell fucking yes!

I was pumped to go. I hadn't gone out during the week in what seemed like an eternity. It'd be a nice break from my usual routine of watching TV and clicking around on a computer. Real live human interaction with my peer group? Sure, let's do it. Game nights are always a good time. That's practically a fact. What better way to feel like a carefree young'un than by tossing some dice or shuffling a deck of cards with good company? It's about as wholesome as you can get; it's practically a slice of Mom's apple pie via an Evite link. Personally, I love a good game night, and I've never turned an invitation down. Why should I? It's practically free fun.

Alvin lived in Fishtown, which is a neighborhood in North Philadelphia in the process of being gentrified. All the artsy kids were moving in and setting up community gardens and cramped coffee shops with rickety wooden chairs. You know the drill.

I'd been to Alvin's house once before when he had a Memorial Day barbecue last summer. He was dating my friend Tia so I popped in on a whim. From what I remembered, it was a great party. His backyard patio was illuminated by strings of colored Christmas lights that cast a lovely glow over everything. I kissed a dude named Dudley at the end of the night on Alvin's front porch. Dudley asked if I wanted to go back to his place two blocks away, right by the beer distributor, but he accidentally belched right in my face while he was in the middle of propositioning me. I must've been downwind because I got a faceful of his beer burp. I waved my hand a bit to disperse the noxious cloud while he slurred an apology, but the damage had been done. The mixture of his Budweiser burp with the humid summer air made me want to run home and squirt Purell all over my body. Yeah, I turned him down. Sorry, Dudley.

Also from what I remember, Alvin was a great host, circulating around the party to make sure everyone was having a good time. At one point during the night, he tried to breakdance in the middle of his living room, which I thought was pretty cool. I had run into him a few times since then, and I was excited that he'd thought to invite me to his game night. We had a few friends in common and—I'm not going to lie—I was excited to get out of my parents' house for the evening.

I swung by Alvin's place at seven P.M. on the dot because I'm overly punctual. He greeted me at the door.

I looked at him standing in the doorway at an adorable 5'7". He was wearing a red plaid flannel shirt and dark blue jeans, which made him look like a lumberjack. As I leaned in to hug him, I took a whiff of his shirt and I was pleasantly surprised at how lovely it smelled. Creepy girl confession: One of my favorite things about life is going in to hug a guy I like and smelling his clean, crisp T-shirt. When I get a nostrilful and it smells like skipping through an Irish meadow on a spring day, I want to high-five myself, high-five him, and high-five his washing machine and dryer.

I don't know if he washes his laundry with crack or what (does crack even smell good?), but I cannot get enough. And just knowing that his shirt is going to be in my life for the next two to twelve hours—if it goes well—puts a pep in my step. Let's put it like this: If a guy's shirt smells like a corsage on prom night, then I'm going to keep him around as long as possible.

On the flip side, if a guy has terrible-smelling clothes and I'm bitch-slapped by his B.O. when I go in for a hug, I don't care how extensive his record collection is, how many funny videos he forwards to me while he's at work, or how cool his sneakers are; he has a zero percent chance of making it past a third date. Them's the breaks! It's "clean shirt or bust" up in here.

There have been a few rare occasions when a guy smells like nothing, and that really throws me off my game. I'll be in his closet sniffing his sweaters when he leaves the room to pee. I'm like Scully rifling through his X-Files. Why doesn't this guy smell like anything? Is he a ghost? Am I on a date with Powder? I get all existential about it. If his shirt doesn't smell like anything while it's on his body, was the shirt even on?

But Alvin? Goddamn! I wanted to package his shirt's scent and pop it in the wall as my air freshener. I wanted to snuggle up in his armpit and hang out for a little while. Maybe build a pillow fort with his shirt as the roof. Maybe just lie around and finish a crossword puzzle, stopping every few minutes when I'm trying to think of a word to roll over and catch a whiff. It was like catnip to me.

I was surprised that we hadn't hooked up yet because now that I got a good look at Alvin, he was totally my type. In both looks and personality, he was a solid guy. His body was shaped like a mug of beer: thick everywhere from top to bottom. One could describe him as being husky. I mean, he was the catcher on his softball team. Those are the sturdiest guys ever by nature. I normally don't go for guys my friends have dated, but they only dated for two weeks over a year ago and she ended it because he was too short for her. I was sure she wouldn't mind if I took a crack at him.

"Welcome to my humble abode." He made a sweeping gesture, one a wizard might make.

"Yeah, man. Thanks for having me."

"Come in, come in." As I stepped inside, I ran smack into the handlebars of his bike, which was leaning against the wall of his foyer. I instinctively clutched my purse because it felt like the bike was trying to pick my pocket as I walked to the living room.

"Ooh! Watch your step," he warned, but it was already too late; his bike was attacking me. The handlebars—or, as I like to call them, the ovary-impalers—jabbed at me as I squeezed by. The pedals stabbed at my shins like a teensy ninja. Seriously, fuck this fucking bike in his fucking hallway.

I know there's nowhere else to stash the thing because we live in a city and it'd probably get stolen in about half a minute if he locked it to a tree outside, but it doesn't mean that I should have to endure this pat down courtesy of his ten-speed.

"It's fine. I got it," I said, scooting past as quickly as possible. I had to suck in my stomach for a split second to make it past.

Aside from the bike feeling me up in the hallway, his house was exactly as I'd remembered it. It was definitely a dude's house. There was clunky, dusty artwork that looked like it'd been salvaged from a yard sale nailed to the dark red walls. Stacks of records were lined up against one side of the wall where the stereo was set up. He had a large, brown sofa that you could tell from across the room was going to be a comfortable seat. And he had a few wooden chairs fanned out as auxiliary seating for the game night crowd.

Then, like the cavalry charging from the distance, came the clickity-clack of several sets of paws running full-speed toward me. Before I knew what was happening, three boisterous dogs surrounded me and acted like they lived to shove their nose in my bathing suit area. A trio of cold noses plunged into my crotch like I had stashed Beggin' Strips in my Levi's. If these dogs were on Facebook, I'm positive that they'd list "smelling strangers' crotches" in their interests. If they subscribed to magazines, I'm sure that they'd subscribe to *Crotch Aficionado Monthly*. They certainly didn't hide their enthusiasm that I was there.

Thanks to my catlike reflexes, I was able to block their torpedo noses with my hands as Alvin yelled and clapped loudly, "Come on, get down. Chopper, Zeke, Matilda: Leave her alone." None of those dog names rolled off the tongue easily, but they seemed to fit such a motley crew of four-legged beasts perfectly. They were mutts, so I had no idea what kinds of dogs they were, but they were the kinds that loved crotches, apparently.

Alvin came over and yanked them off me, grabbing their collars as they scratched at my legs. Streams of drool poured out of their mouths, streaking my jeans with glistening saliva.

"Go on, get on your beds!" he yelled. The scampered away without protest.

"I'm so sorry about these guys," Alvin apologized. "They're animals."

I tried to wipe the drool off my pants, but it just smeared around more. "Don't worry about it," I said, making a face at the slime on my legs.

"Here, let me take your stuff." I handed him my coat and purse, which he stashed in his closet out of reach of the mutt circus. Then, I handed him the six-pack of beer I'd brought. His face lit up as he took the beers back to the kitchen to toss in the fridge.

"Wait! I'll have one." I reached over and plucked a bottle out of the pack and twisted off the cap. After being attacked by both a bike and a pack of wild animals, I needed a beer.

A bunch of people came after me, all bundled up in turtleneck sweaters and wool cardigans. After watching the rest of his guests get mauled by the hyper dog parade, Alvin herded us into his living room with a "Let's get this party started already!"

He stood in the center of the room with his arms full of colorful board games. He plopped them down on the coffee table as we all looked on.

"Okay. We've got Apples to Apples, Cranium, Monopoly, and a few editions of Trivial Pursuit. Which one do you guys wanna play?"

After a quick deliberation, we decided on Trivial Pursuit, 90's Edition. I had never played it before, so I was excited to test my nineties knowledge. I took a pull from my beer as I looked around the room. It felt lovely to sit around with some buddies for game night. *We should really make this a regular thing,* I thought.

I was also having a great time flirting with Alvin. We played on the same team, so it was us against three other teams of two. I wanted the Kurt Cobain-y game piece so we went with that.

One team took the Palm Pilot one. One team took the computer monitor with *dot.com* on it. The last team begrudgingly played the cappuccino game piece. Each team was given a small plastic brown wheel. As you answered questions from different trivia categories correctly, you received a colored plastic wedge, with the color corresponding to the trivia category. Once your brown wheel filled up with all the colored wedges, you won. After a few rounds, we quickly realized that either we were all gifted geniuses about the 1990s or the questions were too easy.

- "What sitcom star popularized the Rachel haircut?"
- "What movie has Billy Crystal say of tough guy Jack Palance, 'Did you see how leathery he was?'"
- "What real Seattle band was featured as the rockers Citizen Dick in Cameron Crowe's film *Singles*?"

I could've been in a coma during the nineties and answered those questions correctly. Alvin sat next to me on the wooden chairs and our knees touched a few times, which I liked. As we drank more, friendly trash talk between the teams escalated.

"There's no way that you know this one. Give it up, dude," I ribbed this short girl with glasses named Lizzy.

"The answer's Pearl Jam, mutherfucka. Booyah! *Give me my wedge.*" She triumphantly jammed an orange wedge in her wheel, then high-fived her teammate.

It was our turn next and our question was a real tough one:

- "What film suspended production for a year so Tom Hanks could let his hair grow and lose 50 pounds?"

"You got this one?" Alvin asked me.

"Totally, The movie's *Cast Away*, bitches! Now gimme my wedge."

Lizzy confirmed my answer with a nod and placed the trivia card back in the pile. I stood up to grab my orange wedge from a tall skinny dude named Lance who kept the plastic bag of wedges. I even did a little dance as I retrieved it to rub my victory into the other teams' faces.

As I sat down in my chair, I heard a loud crack and fell backward to the floor. I had broken the chair. I didn't just break it; I decimated it. I went full-on Godzilla on the thing. It totally fell apart, like I was Chris Farley in an SNL sketch, which, I'll admit, did go along with the nineties theme of the night. All the wedges in my stupid wheel went flying onto the carpet. The dogs started freaking out and they ran over to sniff me because that seems like all they ever want to do. Everyone was cracking up while asking if I was okay. I was laughing, too, because what the fuck? I just busted Alvin's chair and now I was being trampled by a pack of dogs. One of them licked my face, which made me wince.

"Oh my God. I'm so sorry, Alvin. I'll, I'll buy you a new one," I stammered in between batting away their floppy tongues.

"Don't sweat it. That chair sucked and it was only, like, ten dollars from IKEA." He was being a good sport even though he was dying laughing like everyone else in the room. He finally pulled the dogs off me.

Who breaks a chair like that? What's wrong with me? Of the top five most embarrassing things you can do in front of a guy you like, breaking a chair must be numbers two through five. I'm not sure what the number one thing would be but I'd imagine it'd be menstruation related. At least I didn't get my period on the broken chair. That'd be worse.

Once we all settled down and he got me a seat with a sturdier frame, I pulled Alvin into me.

"I cannot believe that just happened," I whispered.

"Oh man, I have to hand it to you: That's the funniest thing I've seen in forever."

"I am *mortified!*"

"Don't be! Seriously. It's fine," he said.

I covered my face with my hands.

"I swear to God, you're overreacting. It's *fine.*"

"I'm totally embarrassed, you guys," I announced to the room. They all told me that it wasn't too big a deal.

"Really, Anna. Don't worry about it," Lizzy said. Fuck. I needed another beer after that. I got up to retrieve another from the fridge.

The game raged on, with us duking it out for nineties trivia superiority. We won a round and the cappuccino team won the other. After my fourth beer and third round of the game, I realized that I was getting pretty tipsy. I knew that I'd have to drive back to my parents' house in a bit, so I went to the kitchen to pour myself a glass of water. Alvin followed me.

"Hey," he said as we entered the kitchen.

"Oh, hey! I'm grabbing some water. I hope that's okay."

"Yeah, sure. No problem. Here, let me get that for you." He reached for a glass in his cabinet. "You're not heading out just yet, are you?"

"Well, I have to drive home later, so I don't wanna get too drunk," I explained as he turned on the sink faucet. The water hissed into the glass.

"Who says you have to go home?" He raised an eyebrow.

Alvin was making a move on me.

"Really? You wanna have a slumber party with me?" A slumber party? Who says that? What am I, twelve?

"Yeah, that could be fun." He leaned in to kiss me, but I put my hands on his chest to stop him.

"What are we talking about here? A few rounds of Girl Talk? Truth or dare? Painting each other's nails?"

He laughed. "Something like that."

"So let me get this straight: I broke a chair in your house and you're asking me to stay over?"

"Yeah, I guess I am." His brown eyes softened as they focused on my mouth. I pulled him closer to me and he placed his hands on my hips.

"Are you into chair breakers? Does that turn you on? Is that, like, your fetish?" I joked.

"How about we talk less about you breaking chairs and talk more about you staying over." I laughed while I considered the request for a few more seconds.

"All right. Let's do it." I took my hands off his chest and pulled his face to mine for a quick kiss.

Game night ended pretty quickly after that. Alvin ushered

everyone out, which was fine by me. As soon as the last person thanked him and left, he opened a bottle of Merlot Lizzy had brought and poured us each a glass. After putting some *Pet Sounds*–era Beach Boys on the stereo, he joined me on the sofa. I was going to avoid lounging on rickety wooden furniture from this point out.

"This is better, isn't it?" he said, sipping his wine. "Just us."

I nodded yes at him, and then nodded toward the stereo. "I didn't realize you were a Beach Boys fan."

"There's a lot you don't know about me." He put his arm on the back of the sofa and I leaned into his chest, deeply inhaling his shirt again like a creep.

"Oh yeah? Like what? What don't I know about you?"

"Well, what do you wanna know? I'm an open book." He kissed the top of my head lightly.

"Okay. Let's start with the obvious: What kind of name is Alvin? I don't know any Alvins. I can say with confidence that you are the only Alvin listed in my cell phone."

"Everyone makes fun of me about it because of the—"

"The Chipmunks, right. Well, Alvin was the coolest chipmunk, so at least you have that going for you."

"It was my grandfather's name. Well, that's not true. His name was Aaron and I'm named in memory of him. That's a pretty boring story. What else do you wanna know?" He started to kiss my neck, which shut me up. I turned around and met his lips with mine.

Aside from breaking a chair in front of all of his friends, I was having the time of my life. Being at my parents' house for so long, I hadn't made out with a cute guy in a while. I forgot just how lovely it could be.

Moving back home was alienating. I'd been living in a suburban cocoon filled with strip malls, well-manicured lawns and cable television for over a year. But for those few minutes on Alvin's couch, it felt like I had my old life back. I was in heaven. At least I was until one of his dogs jumped up on the couch, nearly knocking the glass of Merlot out of my hand with his unchecked exuberance. His paws clawed at my sweater and dug into my skin.

I yelped, trying to hold my wineglass out of reach.

That was when I met my Alvin's inner Hulk: "Zeke! What did I tell you? Get the hell off the couch! Get down, now! Bad boy!" As he yanked at the dog's collar, I thought, *Who is this man?* He was a million miles away from the adorable guy who poured me my wine two minutes ago.

"Sorry 'bout that. He knows he's not supposed to jump on the couch." As the words left his mouth, the dog whipped his thick tail toward us, almost knocking Alvin's wineglass out of his hand, too.

"That's it! Zeke, go to your cage. Now! Go on, get!" He stomped over to the cage, locked the mutt in, and then resumed his place on the couch. Thanks to his outburst, his face was now a deep shade of red.

"Whew! Where were we?" He leaned in to kiss me, acting like nothing had happened, like screaming at an animal was as normal as blowing his nose. This Jekyll/Hyde, screamer/wine sipper thing was intense. I was rattled by it. I didn't want to leave because I was already pretty drunk, so I just tried to shrug the dog screamer thing off.

We kissed a bit, stopping only when another of the mutts would come over to sniff my crotch, and then the screaming thing would start up again.

"Matilda! That's it! You're going to your cage now, too." Then he stopped mid smooch and locked up another one.

"Wow. It's starting to get pretty late," I said, glancing at my watch. He looked over at the clock by the television and agreed.

"I should take 'em for a quick walk before we turn in for the night," Alvin said. "Here, have some more wine. I'll be back in a few minutes."

"Sure thing." I watched him round up the pack of animals and they bounced and jerked around, waiting for him to clip their leashes on. Once they left, the house felt eerily quiet. I figured that this would be the perfect time to freshen up.

The bathroom was on the second floor, a few feet from the staircase. I flicked on the light and took pause. I had no idea how an adult human could use that teensy-weensy bathroom. Everything in there was tiny. The sink was the size of a child's shoe and the mirror over the sink was the size of a Pop-Tart. If we were in the Roaring Twenties, fun-loving collegiates would see how many people they could squish in here for fun. Clark Kent probably has more room in a phone booth to change into Superman. I mean, it was small.

Clearly, the name "bath*room*" was a misnomer because there was no way that this should be classified as a full room; it was more of a closet. A bath closet. It was so tight in there that just walking the one foot from the toilet to the sink felt like I was in a Tokyo subway car during rush hour.

The shower curtain looked like a crime scene: It was stained, torn, and somehow rusted. How does plastic rust? The metal hooks on top of it were all scraggly, like old cavities.

There wasn't a proper shower liner, just a thick plastic sheet. It used to be white, but now it was a yellowish-brown shade that could best be described as "heavy smoker's teeth yellow." Shower curtains are, like, a dollar. Couldn't he just grab a new one? I didn't want to touch the thing because it was slimy and I had no idea what kind of toxic stew was growing on it.

And not to be a diva, but his bathroom had the worst overhead lighting I'd ever seen. It was harsh and unflattering, like a Macy's dressing room. I had to shield my eyes from the brightness. There was one bare lightbulb overhead beaming down on me with the focused intensity of an angry teacher. I guess if he was aiming for a bathroom-at-a-gas-station vibe, he'd nailed it pretty well.

I took out my travel toothbrush and spotted his crusty tube of Crest toothpaste. It was the most basic kind you could get: no advanced whitening agents or foaming molecules. It was just a dry, crumbly paste the consistency of caulk and it was as gnarled as the Wicked Witch of the East's feet after Dorothy gets the ruby slippers in *The Wizard of Oz*. How does a toothpaste tube even get that funky? Maybe a mouse uses it as a punching bag? Maybe it was in a crash test dummy's pocket? Who knows? I had no clue why it was so mangled.

Of course, it had a twist-off cap, which was the Monopoly

game piece of his bathroom; it somehow managed to get lost pretty much within thirty seconds of my touching it. Was it too much to ask for a flip-top cap? And did the flavor have to be an unappetizing flavor of chalk? Couldn't he opt for a Vanilla Mint or a Crystal Wintermint? And it didn't instill confidence that the ingredients were listed in Spanish. Did he fish this out of a Chinatown Dumpster or did he go to an actual store and pay for this with American cash?

I put the tiniest smudge of toothpaste on the outermost bristles of my toothbrush and tried to repress my gag reflex as I smeared it on my teeth. And, to add insult to injury, I had to stand in the hallway to brush my teeth because there was no place for my arms to operate in that cubic foot of terribleness. I was inadvertently doing the Hokey Pokey just trying to get my teeth clean. Somehow my breath managed to smell even worse after I'd brushed my teeth. Disgusted, I cupped my hand under the faucet and sipped some water, swished it around my mouth, and spit it out. Yuck.

I realized that I should probably pee now before he got back, but even that was a nightmare. I was basically peeing in a dollhouse. One knee was hitting the sink and the other knee was slammed against the edge of the bathtub. One elbow was smashing into the wall and the other elbow was tangled in a shower curtain. I'm pretty sure I pulled a muscle just trying to wedge myself on that toilet.

Sorry to be TMI, but I also had to change my maxi pad real quick and, to my horror, he had a tiny wastebasket. With just two Q-Tips, four cotton balls, an empty toilet paper roll, and a used Kleenex, it was already at maximum capacity. The grocery store bag he used for a liner was too big and it slumped over the sides like it hated its life. Honestly, I don't blame it. That trash bag probably envisioned itself growing up to cart some lady's fresh groceries home from Whole Foods, not playing makeshift garbage bag in a guy's rank bathroom.

But the *worst* part was that I had to stash my maxi pad in this overgrown mess. I tried to jam it in the toilet paper roll and placed it in the offending trash can.

I went to wash my hands and was horrified to find a cracked, hardened bar of soap chillin' on the edge of the sink. It had more streaks in it than the quad on campus during homecoming week. Lathering was out of the question; there was no lather left in it. I wondered how soap could get so dirty when it's soap! What do you use to clean soap?

Just so we're clear, I hated this bar of soap. I refused to use it. I thought about putting it out of its misery (i.e., throwing it out), but I couldn't tell if that'd be weird. I set it back on the counter and did my best to forget I ever saw it.

When I was done, I stashed my purse back in the closet and sat on the couch, waiting for Alvin to return. And he did a few minutes later with his menagerie in tow. He instructed them to go to their doggy beds, which they did. It felt like we were babysitting.

I followed him up to his room and we got right down to business. We made out for about an hour. That part ruled. You might be happy to know that he had great armpit hair. I was pleased with this development because a guy's armpit hair is always a crapshoot. You never know what you're going to get. Maybe they'll be thick and smelly, like unruly pubes. Or, maybe he won't have any at all; his skin will just be totally hairless and slightly damp, like a cat's nose. But Alvin, he's got the perfect armpit hair composition. Thin, wispy, soft: This is some Grade A armpit hair, my friend.

I wanted to weave it into braids. I wanted to make a stuffed animal out of it and give it to a sick child. I wanted to kiss it and whisper Laffy Taffy jokes to it and be best buds with that lovely perfect tuft. His awesome armpit hair was excellent news. Just excellent!

We drifted off to sleep shortly afterward with his arms around me. However, I was awakened in the middle of the night by a gnawing sound. I could tell that something was in our room. I rubbed my eyes and tried my best to focus on the small, dark shape squatting by the door. Since I didn't have my contacts in, it took a bit longer to make out what it was. Well, it turned out that it was Zeke, lying down and eating the fuck out of my used maxi pad. He must've fished it out of the trash while we were sleeping.

I gasped and tried to push Alvin awake. "Oh my God! Wake up!"

"What's the matter?"

I didn't say anything; I just pointed at the dog. His eyes followed my finger to the dark shape by the doorway.

"Is that Zeke?" He strained to listen to the horrible chewing sounds. "What's he eating?"

"I think your dog is chewing my pad," I whispered.

"Your what? What'd you say?"

"My pad! *My pad!* Your dog is eating my pad." There are a few words that I hate saying in the company of men. *Tampon* is up there. *Period blood* is on the list, too. But, out of everything, *pad* is number one. No one needs to hear it in a normal tone of voice, much less screamed at them at three A.M.

Alvin leaped out of bed. "Here, boy! Give me that!" He managed to grab a corner of the pad, but Zeke didn't want to give up his bounty right away. He sneered and bared his sharp teeth, which were firmly clenched on the thing.

The good news: I'm sure the dog's saliva was being absorbed well by his new chew toy. The bad news: I wanted to die from embarrassment for the second time in one evening.

Alvin finally managed to wrangle the pad from his pet and promptly disposed of it in the trash can under his desk on the far side of the bedroom. After he put Zeke in his cage, he came back to bed.

"I'm really sorry," I mumbled. Hallmark doesn't make a "Sorry Your Dog Ate My Pad" card, do they? I bet 1-800-FLOWERS doesn't make a "Let's Pretend Your Dog Never Chewed Up My Feminine Product" bouquet, either.

"Don't worry about it. Just go back to sleep." He pulled the covers up to his chest and immediately passed out.

I rested my head on the pillow, but I couldn't sleep. I was horrified. I tossed and turned for a few minutes, totally ashamed. Damn his tiny wastebasket! As I thought about setting it on fire or running it over with my car, I heard a familiar sound. It was the same kind of gnawing, the same kind of panting. I sat up and saw Chopper fishing around the wastebasket. I swear to God, this pad was like Christmas morning for those animals! It was the best thing that ever happened to them since my crotch walked through the door.

So now Chopper got hold of my shredded pad and decided to go to town on it like it was his birthday dinner. I pushed Alvin awake. Again.

"Dude, now Chopper is doing it, too."

"Huh?" He groaned.

"My pad! Chopper is chewing on it, too."

He whipped the sheets back and stomped over to the dog. Chopper thought they were playing a game, so he hopped up on the bed and jumped all over me, his paws stabbing at me like furry daggers. Let me tell you, having a huge dog jump on your seminaked body hurts like a motherfucker. I tried to grab the pad and managed to get a decent grip on it, but the dog wouldn't give it up. He stood his ground, whipping his neck back and forth with more resolve at each tug I made. Large pools of drool streamed from his mouth and sprayed around the room as he twisted his head around. Some of it got in my hair; a speck of it landed on my chin. I was being doused with dog drool.

Finally Alvin managed to snatch the pad from the second pair of teeth that night and locked the dog in his cage, too. All the dogs were barking like maniacs. I heard Alvin rifle around his room looking for something to toss my stupid pad in. He finally found a plastic bag and shoved it in, rolled it up, and placed it on top of his closet, out of reach of doggy teeth. I'm glad the lights were off so he couldn't see the look of abject horror on my face.

Alvin resumed his place on his side of the bed and didn't say anything to me.

"I'm . . . so sorry," I said.

"Don't worry about it. Just go back to bed."

"Not to be a burden, but do you have a towel I could borrow? I'm, like, drenched in dog drool."

With a huff, he got up and trotted to the bathroom. He came back with a small blue towel, which he tossed toward me. "Here you go."

"Thanks." Wait, I'm supposed to dry my body with this? I used his stamp-sized mini-towel begrudgingly. It was all matted and scratchy like a homeless man's dreadlock. And it didn't even do a good job at drying me! Rather, it just pushed the drool around and scratched my skin. It was starting to hurt. I tossed it on the floor like it was rotten.

Alvin managed to catch some Zs. I could tell by his snoring that the pad attack didn't disrupt his beauty sleep. Unfortunately, I barely slept one wink. I kept hearing the dogs whimper in their cages, frustrated that they couldn't play with their new, prized toy. Just as the sun was starting to poke through his curtains, I finally managed to get some shut-eye.

Around ten A.M., we woke up. He didn't mention anything about the pad chase of the night before, which I appreciated. I hoped he forgot the whole thing even happened. The best-case scenario would be him just thinking that it was a vivid nightmare. I certainly wasn't going to bring it up. When he left the room to take a quick shower, I found the pad and tossed it in my purse. I was hoping that if he did go to look for it after I left and didn't find it, he'd definitely think that it was a nightmare.

After a quick cup of coffee, I gathered my things and left. The brisk winter morning air felt like it was punching my wine hangover in the face. I squinted in the sunshine. My armpits stank and there was dog drool still in my hair. And I was pretty sure that I wasn't going to be invited to any more game nights at Alvin's place. Between his bike getting to first base with me, his dogs getting to second, and him rounding third, I figured it was time for me just to go home. All I wanted was to take a nice, long shower, then crawl into bed.

When I got home, I saw that my mom was on the phone. She looked at me and said, "It's okay, Officer. She's here. In fact, she just walked through the door." I guess you know the rest.

CHAPTER 3

# Short Guys Rule

Hello! Is this thing on?" [*taps microphone*] "Can you guys hear me in the back? You can? Okay, cool. My name is Anna and I am addicted to short guys. It's something I struggle with on a daily basis. I've tried to overcome it; I've tried to get into guys with longer inseams. But short guys just feel so good, you know? To hug them, to kiss them, to feel them against me. I love their little hands and their little feet. Oh God. I feel a relapse coming on. Let's wrap this up. There are doughnuts and coffee by the door. Thanks for coming."

Well, it turns out that there isn't a recovery group for people who prefer men under 5'8". I'm in a true minority, like Inuits or full-time mimes. I have never met another woman who has told me that she prefers shorter men. Usually, women are resigned to it: "Eh, Lewis is a great guy. I just wish he were a little bit taller." I have never said that.

As soon as I walk into a room, I scan the joint for the shortest guy to hit on. Sometimes I feel like I'm the only one who knows just how radical they are. Maybe loving short guys is a cult phenomenon, like attending midnight showings of *The Rocky Horror Picture Show* or caring about the plot of *Donnie Darko*. Maybe it takes a special kind of woman to prefer their shorter limbs, if not downright demand them. I am that special woman.

How much do I love them? Well, let's put it like this: When people asked me what I wanted for my birthday last year, I told them that I wanted a harem of eight guys under 5'8": one for each day of the week and an alternate in case one of them got sick. My friends chuckled uncomfortably because they knew that a harem of short guys would be my ultimate birthday present, but it would probably involve a Craigslist post to get the ball rolling, and no one wants to sort through the e-mails to organize that.

When I tell people that yes, I'm a 6'1" woman who would rather date a short dude, they look at me like I'm clinically insane. They have no idea why I'd rather snack on a fun-sized Snickers bar when there are king-sized Snickers bars out there. *Because a fun-sized Snickers feels better in my boobs!* Wait, that didn't come out right.

I have never been attracted to a guy taller than me. I have never Googled a man over 6'1" to find out more information about him. I have never daydreamed about being somewhere tropical with a guy over 6'1". Honestly, they don't even register on my radar. They're background noise, cluttering up my view, getting in the way. They're redwoods when I'd just prefer a nice shrub.

You might wonder what it is about a shorter man that is so appealing. Well, I love how they have to stand on a curb to kiss me good night. I love how they have to strain their neck to meet my lips. I love how their little hands feel on my long legs. I love it all.

It was a shock when I found out that not everyone feels the same way I do about dating a shorter man. It was a fairly recent discovery. As I started to hook up with more guys in Philly, my friends noticed a pattern emerging. When we'd walk into a party and whisper about the hot guys who turned our heads, I'd consistently swoon over the littlest dudes. We started calling short guys "Anna-boys."

"Oh, that guy is totally an Anna-boy."

"Where?" I looked over at the short guy in a hoodie pulling on a beer in the corner.

"Oh, yeah," I agreed, nodding. "That's a total Anna-boy."

My mother hoped that my attraction to short guys would be a phase that I'd outgrow, like dyeing my hair black or buying clothes at thrift stores. I did outgrow those other things, but as I got older, I liked my men staying the same height, which was approximately as high as my chest.

I feel like the Ghost of Christmas Past here, but let's take a peek at me when I was younger. There I am in second grade at Hebrew School, taller than everyone else at my class, staring at the shortest boy, named Lev. He looked like Fievel in *An American Tail*, all ears and floppy shirts. He was the first boy to give me butterflies in my stomach and the shortest one in my grade. There I am drawing our initials with a plus sign between them, corralled within a heart drawn in red crayon, while he's knocking around with toy trucks on a patch of carpet. He doesn't even notice that I'm transfixed by him.

Those with a heart condition might want to sit down before they read the rest of this sentence, but Lev did not return my affections. I don't even think he ever bothered to learn my name. I guess I wasn't a hot second grader? Maybe my turquoise culottes didn't do it for him? Who knows? But it wouldn't be the last time a short guy had no freakin' clue how to handle my attraction to him.

My next crush ruined me for life: I was in third grade and his name was Michael J. Fox. I was obsessed with Alex P. Keaton from *Family Ties*. I was a tall, awkward nine-year-old and he was a short, jittery Republican who constantly ran his hands through his feathered hair; clearly we were a match made in heaven. I'd kiss the television when he'd be onscreen, wiping away the dust on my lips with the back of my hand.

My sister Sarah would recoil every time I did it, but I didn't think it was gross. He was my man. Of course we'd kiss! Unfortunately, it didn't feel like kissing him even though our lips were so close. As my hand smeared with soot reminded me, I was kissing dusty glass, not his perfect lips.

For my birthday that year, my mother took me and my sisters

to see *Back to the Future* at the movie theater. Marty McFly was the hottest guy I'd ever seen in my life up to that point. Those tight jeans! Those suspenders! *Those purple Calvin Kleins!* I didn't even know guys' underwear came in purple; talk about a game changer. I wondered what his neck smelled like and what it'd feel like to squeeze his thigh the way Lorraine did under her parents' dining-room table. I wanted him to gaze at me the way he gazed at a 4x4 truck at the end of the film. I wanted to know. I *needed* to know.

After I saw the movie, I plastered my walls with Michael J. Fox posters that I'd eagerly tear out of *Teen Beat* magazines. I had him "in stereo," smiling at me from all sides of my bedroom. Dozens of Michaels, all hovering over me like an attentive, friendly boyfriend. I knew he was out of reach, like all teen heartthrobs. He lived in Hollywood; I lived in a shitty small town outside Albany, New York. And, given our drastic age differences, I'd say our romance was a long shot.

My family moved to the North Shore of Chicago the summer before eighth grade and that's when I started to dig my heels into the music scene. I'd read *Spin*, *Alternative Press*, and *Rolling Stone* from cover to cover. By junior year of high school, I was heading downtown to catch local punk bands playing at the Fireside Bowl every weekend. And that's when I spotted Charlie leaning against a wall. He was 5'6" and something about him reminded me of Michael J. Fox. Maybe it was the way his hair flopped by his ears. Maybe it was the way he jammed his hands in his front pockets the way Marty McFly did. I'm not sure, but I was hooked. I gave him my phone number and instructed him to call it. The first time we talked on the phone, we gabbed for hours. We were inseparable after that.

On our first date, I asked if he cared that I was so much taller than him. He shrugged and said that he thought it was cool. It wasn't like he enjoyed my height; he just seemed not to mind it. That was progress, I guess.

The only time our height difference was ever an issue was when we went to senior prom and he didn't want to slow dance with me because he said that we'd look ridiculous. I nagged him about it until he relented. I have to admit, we probably did look ridiculous with his hands lightly resting on my hips and my arms on his shoulders like a trapezoid in formal attire. But it was freakin' prom! We paid, like, a hundred dollars to go. I had shaved my legs. We were going to dance, goddammit! Well, I got my wish and it was easily the most awkward twelve measures of "End of the Road" by Boyz II Men I've ever danced to.

He looked like he was in physical pain swaying around the dance floor with me for that one minute. He hated it. I watched him hate it and it made me feel bad. So when he asked if I'd had enough before the first chorus even kicked in, I said sure. We went back to our table and joined the rest of our friends. That was the first time that a short guy seemed to love me in private but seemed uncomfortable with the arrangement in public. We held hands under the table for a few minutes and left shortly thereafter.

Most people don't understand the attraction I have to short men. I've had people berate me, suggest psychological counseling, you name it, all because I like shorter dudes. On a certain level, I understand the outrage. You never see taller girls with short guys in the movies unless it's an ugly homeless man who suddenly wins the lottery and decides to surround himself with buxom Amazon women. Usually a shorter man dating a taller woman is a punch line.

But nothing depresses me more than seeing a short guy with a shorter girl. It stings, like he personally rejected me. I imagine him with a huge checklist of qualities that his dream girl would have and he took out a gigantic marker and crossed off "being tall" with gusto.

Don't tell anyone, but I've even cried about being dumped for a shorter girl. The first time it happened was in college after Jason, a 5'5" cutie, ended it with me and picked a girl who was about 5' even. I sobbed into my pillow because I was convinced that no short guy would ever love me. I was a victim of his insecurity, rejected because of my height even though I loved him because of his. I stopped crying after a while, but I felt bad for weeks.

What a cruel fate! Did my mom piss off a wicked witch when I was born? I was like Sleeping Beauty, except instead of her curse of falling asleep at sixteen if a prince didn't kiss her, I'd have to endure watching guys I loved choose other, shorter women. My curse was decidedly worse.

Maybe you're wondering how shorter guys feel about me liking them so much. Confusion, intimidation, bewilderment:

All of those words come to mind. Some take offense, arguing with me that they're not short. This one guy, Ted, who I went out with twice four years ago, snapped at me that his height was "average." Sorry, Ted, but being 5'8" is considered short when I'm 6'1".

And I didn't realize that the word *short* was so charged. It really seemed to bother him like I'd said he was *husky* or *illiterate*. Sheesh. But I *like* short guys, I protested! I'd jump up and down about it on Oprah's couch like Tom Cruise if I could.

I think these guys aren't used to being desired. They aren't prepared for it, frankly. This has happened a million times: I'll see a cute guy at the bar. We'll make eye contact. Then, I'll do that thing where I beckon him with my "come hither" finger. His eyebrows nearly fly off his head as he points to his chest. "Me?"

"Yes, *you!*" I'll confirm with a smile. It's around then that the sweat beads materialize on his forehead. I swear that I can hear him gulp from across the crowded bar. "Yes, short dude in the cool sneakers and V-neck sweater, I want to talk to you."

He seems terrified, like I'm about to yell, "Psych!" if he takes the bait. He looks around the room like he's being punked. Like Ashton Kutcher's going to jump out of a closet and tell him to look in the monitor and wave because, yeah, no tall girl would ever consciously want to date him.

Some short guys *love* the attention I lavish on them. However, I've come to realize that they don't love the attention that they get from everyone else when we go out together. Everyone stares, evaluating the match. Guys are generally insecure anyway, but add an *American Idol*–esque judging experience every time we enter a restaurant and it's enough to make him pick a shorter, less attention-grabbing companion for the next weekend.

Believe me, I've tried to date taller guys. I dated a guy last year named Jack who was 6'4". I'm going to be honest: I can kind of see the appeal of a higher gent. There was less awkwardness. It was nice to lift my head up to kiss him. It was nice to curl up in the crook of his armpit as we watched movies on his couch. And it was nice how his arms wound around my waist when we'd hug. We fit perfectly in a way.

But when it came time to getting it on, it wasn't on. He had such long limbs. And big feet. It was like scaling Mount Rushmore just trying to hook up. He seemed so far away, even when we were close. Honestly, it made me wish he were just shorter. Then he'd be right there, closer to kiss, totally wrapped up in my arms. It'd be way hotter.

I've finally accepted this preference of mine. I'll probably always get weird looks when I walk with a short guy on my arm, but I don't care. I'll be too preoccupied thinking about getting him to stand on a curb for my good-night kiss.

# CHAPTER 4

# Never Trust a Jazz Hound

Moving to New York City to attend Barnard College in the summer of 1996 was a dream come true. It was my first choice of schools and I was elated when I got in. In my mind, New York was the place to be; it was where things happened, the center of the world. All the best bands played there, all the best food was there, it was in the middle of everything, and I felt like it was where I needed to be. It never occurred to me to live anywhere else. I was as wide-eyed as ever rolling into Morningside Heights on a balmy August day with all of my possessions stashed in a ratty suitcase I'd received as a bat mitzvah present from a distant relative.

However, one thing I hadn't planned on was the fact that living in New York made me more uptight than ever. From the beginning, Barnard did a great job of freaking us out about the "dangers" of living in the city. They stuffed our orientation folders full of pamphlets that warned us about pretty much everything we could encounter. As a result, I was terrified of contracting an STD, walking by myself at night, having someone slip something in my drink, and getting mugged, possibly all at the same time. Stomping around Chicago in high school made me cocky because it was my home turf. But living in Manhattan seemed like the real deal, and I was too freaked out to let my guard down. I took everything very seriously. You kind of have to when you're stepping over homeless junkies to walk into your dorm room.

So I didn't drink at all in college. It didn't appeal to me. I was too nervous about "losing control" and "not being aware of my surroundings." Thanks a lot, after-school specials and scary pamphlets! I didn't drink or do drugs in high school and it didn't appeal to me. Plus, being broke, I didn't want to spend the sparse money I did have on alcohol. I didn't see the value in it. To me, it felt like buying cocktails was essentially flushing my money down the toilet.

And, for living in one of the biggest cities on the planet, I surprisingly didn't have a lot of chances to hook up. I didn't hit it off with any guys at school. I was an awkward, music-obsessed nerd with no idea of how to do casual hookups. I was basically a Jewish nun.

Part of the problem was that none of the guys I met at school turned my head. I was starting to think that something was wrong with me. Sure, you don't meet a ton of guys when you attend a women's college, but the guys milling around at Columbia University across the street weren't attractive to me at all. They wore pleated khakis and bragged about where they "summered."

The only guy I liked during college was this 5'5" cutie named Davy Baxter but I was unable to capture his attention. I'd try to strike up a conversation with him, and he'd tune me out. I'd lean over to let him look down my shirt, and he'd look away, totally uninterested. I'd strip naked and hump his acoustic guitar, and he'd just shrug. (Okay, maybe I didn't do that. But if I had, I don't think it would've made a difference.) I finally gave up after a while because my buddy Oliver broke the news to me that he had an Asian fetish and that it was never going to happen between us. I was crushed.

There are several things in life that I know I will never be able to compete with: professional poker players, Michael Phelps in the four-hundred-meter breaststroke, and Asian girls to a guy with an Asian fetish. He wants Lucy Liu and I'm more like Lucy Lawless. It's not going to happen! So I gave up on ol' Davy Baxter. Deprogramming him from his Asian fetish sounded like too much work for me anyway.

To be fair, I probably wasn't a prize back then, either. I went through a phase where I wore camouflage cargo pants all the time. I wore sensible footwear. I didn't own one dress. Now that I think about it, I probably could've used an intervention for that. Where were my loved ones then to tell me about proper eyebrow grooming and the fact that the only girls wearing sneakers who get hit on are girls in cute gym clothes, not hardcore punk band T-shirts? I hadn't figured out how to dress like the kind of woman who was interested in hooking up, so that could've been a factor here.

The universe took pity on me and finally presented me with a make-out opportunity my sophomore year of college. I owe it all to my friend Ricky. We met because in the first semester of my freshman year, I had a radio show at Barnard. Ricky also had a show and we were scheduled during the same time slot but on alternate weeks, so we had to coordinate our schedules together over the phone. What started as a logistical need to talk quickly grew into a chatty friendship. We'd spend hours talking about our favorite indie bands. When we decided to meet in person, he showed up at my dorm looking like Woody from *Toy Story*, if Woody had listened to Pavement and traded in his embroidered cowboy vest for a rust-colored blazer with brown elbow patches on the sleeves. I knew right away that we'd be good friends.

So, when Ricky invited me over for a party at his dorm, I didn't hesitate. I expected it to be a low-key, Friday night hang. What I didn't expect was meeting Wyatt, an awkward, pudgy aspiring filmmaker. He was Ricky's upstairs neighbor, the Kramer to Ricky's Seinfeld. When Wyatt walked in Ricky's bedroom just as the party started to get fun, I grabbed Ricky's arm and begged him to introduce me. Amused, he said sure.

"Wyatt! Hey, man. Have you met Anna?"

"No, I can't say that I have. Hey, there. My name's Wyatt."

"My name's Anna," I said, flustered.

"I'm gonna go grab a beer in the kitchen. Want one?"

"No, thanks. I don't drink."

"Cool. I'll be right back. Don't go anywhere!"

He came back with his beer a few minutes later and sat down next to me on Ricky's couch. We flirted all night. I learned that Wyatt was a sophomore, like me, and that he hailed from Seattle. Right off the bat, the filmmaker thing impressed me. He also wore black-framed glasses, which he'd nervously push up his nose. As the party began to wind down, I looked at my watch.

"It's getting pretty late," I said. "I think I should probably get going."

"Quick question: Have you ever heard John Coltrane's *A Love Supreme*?"

"Nope. I don't really listen to jazz. I'm more of a rock 'n' roll kind of girl."

"Oh, man, you are missing out! There's no way I'm letting you leave here without listening to some Coltrane. Let's go back to my room upstairs and I'll play you some of his best stuff."

I eagerly accepted his invitation. Seeing as we only had to trek up a flight of stairs, we were at his place in no time.

"My roommates aren't home, so we can be as loud as we want," he said as he unlocked his front door. Once we pushed our way inside, I got a good look at the place. The walls were totally bare except for a *Jaws* poster in the hallway that was affixed with purple pushpins, its corners peeling back. "I'm gonna grab a can of Coke. You want one?"

"Sure. Thanks."

"Cool. My room is the first one on the left. Make yourself at home."

I flicked the bedroom light on, and it cast an eerily blue glow over everything. His room was very small, so small that I hit the bed with the door. One tiny window was cracked open, and it faced a red brick wall. A huge poster from some French film I'd never heard of was taped to the wall near his bed. A small picture of his family was framed on his desk.

I walked over to his closet and sniffed a shirt. It didn't smell like anything. Maybe he was a robot? I considered it briefly, and then dismissed the notion.

I perused the spines on his bookshelf, and each book was radder than the next. Aside from having my AP English syllabus on display, he also had an impressive collection of pop culture standards: *High Fidelity*, *Please Kill Me*, and the complete works of e. e. cummings, my favorite poet. He had a collection of recent fiction and film theory works clustered on one side of the shelf along with thick tomes about the Civil War jammed next to a few graphic novels and comic books, too. As Wayne Campbell from *Wayne's World* would say, "Schwiiiing." Judging by these books, Wyatt was clearly my soul mate.

*Please, please, please let him kiss me*, I prayed to whatever god is in charge of college hookups.

He came in holding two Coke cans, handing me one.

"This is great. I really like your room, Wyatt."

"Thanks. Wait. Let me fix this." He turned on his desk lamp and turned off the overhead light. The softer lighting was welcome. "Ah! That's better." He set his Coke down on his desk and leafed through some records from a crate on the floor before settling on one. I sat on the edge of his bed while he placed a record on the turntable.

"*This* is John Coltrane." He put the needle on the record. The notes filled up his room.

"I can see why you like it so much. It's jazzy." I had no idea what I was talking about. I'd never listened to jazz music before, but I didn't want him to think that I was uncultured. "That saxophone is amazing." He came over and sat next to me. Without saying a word, he leaned in and kissed me. My heart was beating so fast, I'm surprised it didn't explode out of my chest and splatter all over the floor like a dropped plate of spaghetti. Then he kissed me again, this time longer and with tongue.

"I think you should turn off the light, don't you?" I whispered.

"That's the best idea I've heard all day." He got up and did just that. It took a second for my eyes to adjust to the darkness. We kissed for a bit more. It seemed like hours, but it was probably, like, five minutes.

"You can stay over if you want," he said, between kisses.

I didn't even hesitate. "Sure. Yeah. Okay." I kicked off my sneakers and he kicked off his, too. I pulled off my camouflage cargo pants. He pulled off his brown corduroy pants. Once under the covers, things started to heat up a bit. I let my fingers touch his boxer shorts. He touched my bra strap.

"This is so crazy that I came back to your place. I definitely wasn't planning on meeting anyone tonight," I said, still in disbelief that this all was happening.

"I know, me too. It's so cool how you're into music. I really dig that about you."

"Yeah? Well, I really like how you want to be a filmmaker," I gushed.

"Would you ever want to go to a film festival with me?"

"Like, a date?"

"Sure! Why not?"

"Yeah. I'd love to. And I'll take you to some punk shows downtown."

"I'd love that."

"I'd love that, too." We kissed about these plans. My mind did somersaults, trying to figure out what I'd even wear to a film festival. This might precipitate a shopping trip.

"Anna, you're so perfect." He stroked my hair a bit.

"You're perfect, too." I curled into his chest and lightly scratched his arm with my fingernail.

"I have an idea. You're gonna think I'm crazy. But, whatever. Fuck it. I'm just gonna go with this. Anna"—he turned to face me—"will you be my girlfriend?"

"Are you serious, Wyatt?"

"I'm totally being serious right now."

"Yes!"

"Really?"

"Yes! Yes, yes, yes. I'd be happy to." I beamed. We both beamed! We kissed for a while longer before falling asleep in each other's arms.

The next morning, I headed back to my dorm room. It was my first walk of shame and it wasn't so much a walk as a full-on sprint because I couldn't wait to get home and tell everyone I'd ever met that I now had a boyfriend. I rang my parents up first.

"Mom, I'm in love." I went down his stats like I was reading them off a baseball card. "His name is Wyatt and he's my new boyfriend. Real quick: He's from Seattle and he's a film major at Columbia. He likes jazz music and gosh, Coke, I guess? The soda pop not the drug."

"What's his last name? Is he Jewish?"

"I don't know his last name yet but I don't think he's Jewish. Are there Jewish people in Seattle? I think he mentioned something about being home for Christmas, so I don't think he is. Look, I gotta go. I have, like, ten more calls I have to make."

I called my high school friends in Chicago and relayed the news. If I'd had room for it in my modest bank account, I probably would've hired a skywriter to tell the entire city: *"I have a boyfriend! Suck on that, NYC!"*

I tried to take a nap, but I couldn't sleep because I was too excited about Wyatt. He was all I could think about. I met up with Ricky back at his place that night to give him the breakdown.

"Ricky, I have something to tell you." I was too ecstatic to keep still. If I had been a puppy, I would've been wagging my tail.

"Yeah? What's up?"

"You're *not* going to believe what happened last night."

"Did you get mugged?"

"No. Well, I guess you could say that *my heart* got mugged."

"That sounds painful."

"It's not painful. It's wonderful. Ricky"—I took a long pause for maximum drama—"I'm in a relationship with Wyatt."

"No!" he laughed.

"Yes!"

"Get *out* of here!"

"We're, like, in love. I swear to God, we're *soul mates*."

Ricky was skeptical.

"Was he drunk? He must've been drunk. I know Wyatt. He's not the kind of guy to do that."

"He wasn't drunk, Ricky. We talked about it this morning, *before I left*, if you catch my drift." I winked because I'm not subtle.

"I'm telling you that he was drunk. He didn't mean it, Anna. He had, like, six beers last night."

"Goddamn it, Ricky! He wasn't drunk! He had all of his faculties. Just be happy for me. Be happy for *us*."

"Okay. How's this: I'm so happy for you. Wow! This is excellent news."

"I don't care if that was sarcastic, I will pretend that it was sincere." As I relayed to Ricky all about the film festivals I would now attend as Wyatt's girlfriend, Wyatt popped his head in, totally catching me by surprise.

"Oh, hey, you guys. I was just heading out to meet some friends. Ricky, I wanted to say what a great time I had last night at your party."

"Yeah, man. Thanks for coming."

Wyatt turned his attention to me, sitting on the couch. "Oh, hey, Anna." He pushed his glasses up his nose.

"Wyatt! Hey." He looked just as adorable as I remembered. His brown hair was kind of messy. I couldn't wait to run my fingers through it again.

"Actually, Anna, do you have a minute? Can we talk for a second?"

"Of course. Excuse me, Ricky." I raised my eyebrows at him to really hammer it home that Wyatt and I were a real couple so *in his face*! I followed Wyatt into the hallway, smiling. When we were alone, I leaned in for a kiss but was surprised to see him hesitate.

"Ah, my boyfriend's all shy now, is he?"

"Anna, this isn't easy." He took a deep breath. "I have something for you."

"Oh yeah?" I giggled. "Am I going to like it?"

"Uh, probably not?" He reached into his pocket and handed me a small letter sealed in a white envelope. It had my name written on the front in red pen. His penmanship was neat. That made me love him even more.

"What's this?"

"Just read it."

The letter was handwritten on his personal stationery, like an official communication from a high-ranking official. He watched as I read it out loud:

*Dear Anna,*

*Thank you for last night. I had a great time getting to know you. When I asked you if you would be my girlfriend, I totally meant it. For that second, it seemed like the most natural thing in the cosmos to be together as a couple.*

*Now, I feel uncomfortable being yours or anyone's boyfriend.*

*I'm just not ready for that kind of commitment right now.*

*I hope you understand that I can't be your boyfriend, but I can be your friend. And, I plan on being your friend. So punk shows and indie film festivals, here we come. Please get back to me with your feelings and/or thoughts. I just want what is best for both of us. Thank you for understanding.*

*Take care,*

*Wyatt Ackerman*
*212-555-1234*
*493 Carmen Hall*
*1000 Amsterdam Ave.*
*NY, NY 10027*
*Wyatt78@columbia.edu*

"Is this a joke?"

He shook his head no.

"Why did you even ask me to be your girlfriend in the first place if you're not ready to have one?"

He shrugged. "I guess I got carried away last night."

"Wyatt, we don't need to be in a relationship," I reassured him. "Do you just want to hang out and go on a few dates and see how it goes?" That seemed like a reasonable request. I was actually proud of myself for keeping an even keel about this.

He frowned. "No. I think it would be best if we just went our separate ways."

"All right. I mean, I can't *force* you to date me." For a split second, I *did* think about forcing him, but I don't think that I could legally do that. So much for my keel being even. I could feel it starting to sink.

"No, no. I'm just not ready to be with anyone right now. You understand, right?" I didn't say anything. "So, we're good here?"

"I guess, yeah," I reluctantly agreed.

"All right. I'm gonna head out then. Thanks for being so cool about everything."

"Yeah, no problem." I was stunned.

"Take care!" And with that, he turned around and walked out of the building.

I went back to Ricky's room and collapsed on his bed.

"What'd your new boyfriend have to say?"

I buried my head in his pillow. "He dumped me."

"What? I can't hear you with your face in a pillow."

I flopped over onto my back. "Ricky! He dumped me. I have just been dumped. Look at this." I tossed the letter at him and it twirled down to his feet. He read it out loud just as I had done six minutes before. I pulled the pillow over my ears so I wouldn't have to hear it again. When he got to the end, after he read the e-mail address out loud, he laughed his head off.

"Did he have to invoke the cosmos? Really?" I whined.

"Wow. Personally, I liked how he included *all* of his contact information at the end. You know, in case you wanna send him a cookie bouquet or a singing telegram or something."

"The thing that bothers me is, why was he carrying the letter around like that? How did he even know that I was here? Was he hoping to bump into me? Was he breaking up with a bunch of girls named Anna, so he made sure to always have one of those letters on his person? That's so weird, right?"

"Totally," Ricky agreed.

"We didn't even date for twenty-four hours! He really felt the need to break up with me?"

"Look on the bright side: You were right about dating him! I was wrong. Doesn't that make you feel better? You love being right about things."

I got up and grabbed my purse. "I gotta go."

"You're leaving?"

"I don't want to be so close to the scene of the crime. There are too many painful memories here." I looked around his room. "We met in this bedroom. He asked me to go back to his place when we sat on that couch. I think I'm going to be sick."

"Aww, chin up, buttercup."

"I was just dumped, Ricky." I started to cry a little bit. A tear streamed down my cheek. I wiped it away.

Ricky stood up, came over, and hugged me. "I don't think

this actually counts as a dumping. You dated for less than a full day."

"It feels real." I looked at him with huge, wet eyes.

"What's the lesson here?"

I wiped away another tear, then shrugged. "What are you, Danny Tanner giving me a lesson at the end of a *Full House* episode?"

"Just answer the question!"

"I don't know, Ricky. Tell me. What's the lesson?"

"Never trust a white guy who wants to play you jazz records. No good can come from that."

"Don't make me laugh. I'm mourning a loss here."

"I'm serious! Nothing good can come from a jazz hound. That should've been your first clue."

"But I thought saying that you listen to jazz is a shorthand way to say that you are cultured, like that you eat sushi with chopsticks, or you own several Criterion Collection movies on DVD or listen to NPR. People who listen to jazz own tea kettles, Ricky! They wear turtlenecks when seasonally appropriate and they have bookshelves filled with actual books. I thought those were the kinds of guys I wanted to date."

"So I guess this means that you're in the market for a rebound? Yes?" Now he was the one wiggling his eyebrows up and down.

"It took me over a year to find one guy I liked. It'll probably take a dozen more until I find another guy. Fuck everything. I'm going to be alone forever."

"Oh, come on. Now you're just being dramatic."

"We were going to go to film festivals together!" I whimpered. "I had my heart set on it. I even picked out the outfit in my head. Or, at least, I realized I'd have to go shopping for a good outfit."

"I'll go to film festivals with you. Would that make you feel better?"

"A little bit. Promise?"

"I promise."

"All right, I have some phone calls to make."

"Yeah?"

"I gotta tell my parents that I'm single again."

"I'm sure they'll be bummed at the news."

"I also have to call my friends and break it to them. This is going to take a while. I have an entire phone tree to work through. Bye, Ricky. Thanks for the pep talk."

"You'll be okay."

"Thanks, buddy."

As I headed out onto the street, Ricky opened his window and yelled, "Remember: *Never trust a jazz hound!* Write it down if you have to. Only you have the power to prevent falling for a jazz hound."

Lesson learned.

## CHAPTER 5

# It's All in the Details

After the Wyatt debacle, I didn't even so much as kiss a guy again for almost two years. Two years, people! I had resigned myself to the fact that no guy would ever want to date me for the rest of my life. I was convinced of it. As the daughter of a scientist, I looked at the facts, which only supported my hypothesis that I was destined to a life of solitude. My cluelessness about where to meet guys along with my cluelessness about what to do with one if I did bring him back to my lair pretty much pointed in one direction: spinsterhood. Part of me felt like I should embrace my fate, take up knitting classes, and learn to love the exclusive company of cats.

But another part of me was still hopeful that I could figure this puzzle out. I wasn't ready to enter the convent just yet. The main problem was that I wasn't meeting any guys in my classes at school. And I wasn't attracted to any of my guy friends, so they didn't count as viable romantic prospects.

That was where *Details* magazine came in. It was my window to a man's world: how they thought, how they acted, how they dressed. Reading it felt like I was taking a peek inside the guys' locker room. The next best thing I had to a steady man in my life was my monthly subscription to *Details*. At least that came regularly. It's crazy to say, but sniffing the cologne samples on their pages was the closest I got to smelling a real live human man. I read every issue cover to cover, like a Bible with pictures of hot dudes on every other page. I especially enjoyed the articles about sex because although I wasn't having it, I was fascinated by people who did.

Everyone says that your college years are the most carefree, wild times of your life. My college experience was the polar opposite: I was sitting in a dorm room sniffing Polo Sport from a piece of paper trying to experience the thrill of masculinity through osmosis. Put that in your brochure, Barnard.

I didn't even go on a real date until my senior year of college, just a few weeks shy of my twenty-first birthday. The lucky man? A scrappy guitarist named Tommy. His doughy, round body was covered with tattoos, and his black spiky hair was thin yet somehow always oily. Even though he was only twenty-six years old, he had a beer belly, which freaked me out. Apparently, we'd met a bunch of times but I didn't remember the details of those encounters.

So no one was more shocked than me to hear his voice on

the other end of my phone. One bright February day, he tracked down my phone number and called me out of the blue. I was in the kitchen making lunch when he called.

"Hey. Is Anna there?"

"Yeah, this is she," I said, slowly. "May I ask who's calling?"

"This is Tommy!"

"Tommy?" I didn't remember giving my number to anyone named Tommy.

"You know, Trish's friend? I play guitar in Hellbent. We've met, like, a bunch of times before."

"Oh, Tommy! Yeah, I remember you." He could probably hear my wheels turning as I tried to place him.

"Anna, we've met a bunch of times before."

"Really?"

"Yeah. Like, at least five times. Think hard."

"Riiiiiight. Tommy!" I pretended to know who he was to keep things moving. "How'd you get my number?"

"Trish gave it to me. Well, scratch that. I made her give it to me."

"Why'd you do that?"

"Well, I was just wondering what you're doing tonight. I thought maybe we could go out."

"Go out? With me?"

"Yes! Is that weird?"

"No, it's not weird. Let's see. What am I doing tonight? Gosh, nothing?" I twisted the phone cord around my finger. "Is there anything fun going on?"

"Well, there are two parties tonight. One is in Brooklyn.

Some kid I went to school with at NYU named Kyle is having a house party. The word on the street is that it'll be fun. The other party I heard about is in a loft in midtown."

"Okay." I weighed the two parties out in my mind, with no real preference. I was still processing the fact that a guy had called my phone number on purpose. And I was also processing how great his voice was. It was a deep voice, a man's voice. I don't think my phone had ever entertained a voice that deep before. I had to sit down.

"I'm leaning more toward heading to the party in midtown," he said.

"Oh yeah? Why's that?"

"Because it's closer to you."

I blushed so hard that my face got hot. I unzipped my sweatshirt.

"Why don't I swing by your way and pick you up?"

"Up by me? No, I live in Morningside Heights. That's practically Harlem. Where do you live?"

"I'm in Brooklyn. Like, five stops off the L train." I didn't know much about Brooklyn. All I knew was that it was far.

"That's sweet, Tommy, but it'll take you at least forty-five minutes to come up by me. How about I just meet you at the party?"

"Anna, I want to be a gentleman about this. You know, pick you up and stuff." It was nice that he wanted to display any kind of chivalry toward me, but the thought of an awkward subway ride down to the party together seemed like it would make my head explode.

After much protesting on my part, he finally agreed to meet me at the loft party at ten thirty P.M. This was the first date I'd had since high school. I panicked. I hopped in the shower and deforested both my legs and my armpits. For this, my first date of 1999, I settled on dark blue jeans and a fuzzy, tight pink turtleneck that I'd scrounged from a thrift store. That, coupled with my dyed black hair and Betty Page bangs, made me look like an indie rock starlet. The weakest area of my outfit was my footwear, a clunky pair of Merrell hiking boots. It was the only pair of shoes that I owned as I have an aversion to any sort of a high-heel situation. Since my toes are the approximate size and shape of gnocchi, they can't fully support my body when I wear anything higher than a flip-flop. I topple over like Jenga. What my hiking boots lacked in sex appeal, they made up for in comfort, which was great news for running to class, but a bummer when trying to look cute on a first date. I really hoped he wouldn't look at my feet.

After double-checking that I had my keys, wallet, and lipstick, I hopped on the train and headed downtown to meet him.

The party was in a huge loft space where the walls were painted white and neon pink drapes framed the large windows overlooking the city. Everyone stood around and looked bored, which New Yorkers are great at doing. Techno music blasted out of two speakers propped up on one side of the room. I didn't recognize anyone there. I figured Tommy was the guy walking toward me with a wide smile on his face. He was wearing a navy blue hoodie, jeans, a brown wool coat, and had a brown messenger bag slung across his chest.

"Anna! You made it! Did you have any trouble finding the place?"

"Nope. None." I looked him over. Ah, Tommy! Now I remembered meeting him. Sort of.

"Wow! You look ravishing." He scanned me up and down. "Seriously, you're gorgeous." Since I wasn't used to receiving compliments, I decided to argue with him.

"No, I'm not."

"I love that sweater. It fits you perfectly." He reached over and rubbed my sleeve.

"No, it doesn't. In fact, I think it's a little tight."

"Seriously, you look beautiful."

"My hair looks stupid."

"Your coat is great, too."

"I only paid two dollars for it."

"Anna, just say, 'Thank you, Tommy.' Try it."

"Thank you, Tommy," I conceded.

"There. Was that so hard?"

"So, what do you think of this party?"

"Well, I just walked in but so far, it seems okay. Can I get you something to drink?"

"Actually, no, I'm fine." I'm fine.

"You sure? They have an open bar."

"Yeah, really. I'm good."

"Wait, you don't drink, do you?"

I shook my head no. "How'd you know?"

"Trish told me." He'd really done his homework. I was impressed.

"It's all true." I shrugged.

"Well, we'll see how long that'll last once you hang with me."

"Good luck with that. I can't see you breaking me of this nondrinking habit anytime soon."

"So, you don't drink. We can't go to a bar then, can we?"

"I'm only twenty; I couldn't get in even if we did go." I was starting to feel bad. He couldn't take me anywhere.

"Oh shit! I forgot! You're young, too."

I honestly couldn't think of one other place to go. A restaurant? A club? I didn't know of any other parties. Plus, we were in midtown Manhattan where unless you're going to a ballet or a museum, there isn't much to do past eleven P.M. Finally, I suggested, "Do you just want to go back to my place?" His eyes lit up.

"Anna, are you hitting on me?"

"No, I-I . . . just thought that . . ." I stammered. "I mean, if it's too weird—"

"Don't worry your pretty little head about it. Let's go." He took my hand and we left. Normally, I would never take a guy home twenty minutes into our first date, but I had no idea what I was doing. I'm going to plead ignorance on this one. I was just thinking that we'd go back to my room and hang out because that was what I'd done in high school with my boyfriend. I had no idea what Tommy thought my asking him back to my room meant. That stressed me out, too. Did he think we were going to bang? As soon as we stepped foot on the 9 train heading uptown, I started to panic.

Tommy was the first guy I'd ever taken back to my dorm

suite. I shared the spot with four friends. And they were all in the common room eating pizza when I walked in with him.

"Hey, guys. This is Tommy." They mumbled a few low hellos as I pointed each of them out to him. "That's Julie, Kate, Allison, and the one over there is Maria."

"Good evening, ladies." He waved. The room was dead silent. They all exchanged looks. Maria stopped chewing altogether and just had her mouth hanging open in total disbelief that I'd brought a guy home. "We're going to hang out in my room now," I announced.

"It was nice meeting you all," he said as we walked the ten feet to my corner room. That was when I realized that my bedroom was in no condition to entertain a man. I made him stand outside in the hallway as I did a quick five-minute cleanup. I jammed my dirty scattered clothes on the floor into the closet. I straightened up my desk. I made the bed and did a quick spritz of my perfume in the air as a makeshift air freshener. As a final touch, I put a Specials CD on the stereo, you know, to set the mood. Why I picked a ska band, I'll never know. Let's just say that the vibe in my boudoir was definitely upbeat.

"Okay, Tommy. You can come in now," I shouted through the door. He gingerly twisted the doorknob.

"Are you sure it's safe to come in? There's no, like, dead hookers here or anything, right?"

"Nope! I put them in the bathtub. My bedroom's all clear."

"Sweet place!" he said, sizing it up. He looked at the band posters tacked up on the walls and nodded in approval.

"Yeah, I do what I can." He dropped his dirty brown messenger bag in the corner and kicked off his shoes. That was when it became clear to me that he took no pride in his sock situation whatsoever. Not only were his socks mismatched, but they had holes in them. It was like he had no quality control in his foot underwear at all; any old piece of cloth somewhat shaped like a foot must be granted permanent residence in his sock drawer.

Clearly his socks were the fruitcake of his wardrobe. They were probably a present from his aunt or something. And I bet that they would never get tossed out even though they had catapulted past their expiration date. I'd have bet that he needed to give at least seventy-five percent of his sock collection the boot. Instead, he'd just wear them until the threads peeled away from his foot in total despair. The ones he had on his feet were thin, and any trace of elastic had long since abandoned the effort, so they slouched around his ankles like a kid being yelled at by his parents. The holes by the toes were especially pathetic, like his feet were auditioning for the role of Tiny Tim in a community play. I briefly considered passing around a Pepsi can in the common area to scrape up enough money to get him a six-pack of athletic socks at Target.

That was when it hit me that I finally had a guy alone in my room, slouchy socks be damned. It was like having a wish granted by a genie or a charitable foundation. Sure, Tommy wouldn't have been my first choice. Yes, he looked like a warthog, but it was a bit of a beggars/choosers situation and I wasn't going to start splitting oily, black hairs about it. And, I have to say, I was warming up to Tommy. He made me feel pretty.

"So, you're in my bedroom."

"I am."

"What do you want to do? We could listen to some records."

"Actually, I'm starving. Do you have anything to eat?"

"Yeah. Hang out here. Make yourself at home while I fix us some snacks."

"Can I change the music?" I guess the ska wasn't doing it for him.

"Absolutely. Put something nice on."

I saw my roommates on the way to the kitchen and they all basically flipped their lid.

"Who is this guy?" Allison whispered loudly.

"Oh my God, are you guys going to do it?" Maria giggled.

"You're gonna get so much action tonight. Holy shit." Allison was trying to contain herself. Kate pretended that she was humping the air, and then she whispered, "That's totally gonna be you tonight! Ha!"

"Shhhh! Keep it down! He'll hear you. I'll tell you all about it later, I promise." Before I headed back with a few slices of frozen pizza I'd burned in the oven, they all high-fived me like I'd already scored the touchdown. Cool; I had my own cheerleading section.

When I came back, I found him sitting on the edge of my bed playing my guitar. I stood in the doorway for a second, watching him noodle around. He clearly had some chops.

I smiled. "Wow, I didn't know you could play guitar that well. That's great, Tommy." But he didn't stop. He started singing. And that was when it got weird for me.

It was like John Mayer possessed his body or something. He closed his eyes and started hittin' some high notes. When he finally opened his peepers, I think he tried to make meaningful eye contact with me while he was singing.

I didn't expect him to know this since it was only our first date, but I *hate* when people look at me when they're singing. It makes me self-conscious: Should I return this meaningful gaze? Should I sway back and forth with a lighter in the air? Should I burst into tears like a Beatles fan in the sixties? He had just turned my cozy bedroom into open mic night at the Peach Pit. I'd have totally smashed the guitar to put an end to this impromptu serenade like John Belushi did in *Animal House*, except that it was my guitar and, yeah, I wasn't going to do that.

I wondered if this was something he saw in a movie as a slick move to "seal the deal," which made me panic even more. Honestly, I'd have preferred it if he left the singer-songwriter act for the street performers in the park.

But I didn't tell him that. I just waited for him to strum the last note and said, "That was really lovely, Tommy." I handed him his burnt pizza.

"Aw. Thanks, Anna. You're the best. You know I sang that song for you."

Then he kissed me, which I liked so I didn't have to keep babbling about the song he just sang. He forgot all about the pizza I just gave him. He placed it on the floor and pulled me onto my bed. I must say, he wasn't a terrible kisser. It was pretty nice, actually.

"Hey, you can sleep over if you want, but is it okay if we just kiss for now?" It took all of my courage to ask him to stay.

"Of course! I'd really like that."

"Cool." I kicked off my giant shoes and they landed on the ground with a thud. By the time I shimmied out of my turtleneck sweater, he had already peeled off his clothes and was in his boxer shorts. He must be a part-time male-stripper because he just flipped his outfit off in one fluid motion. Then it dawned on me: I had a semi-naked man in my room. Holy shit. His ding-dong was on my twin bed. I wanted to get a commemorative plaque or something. *Here lay a man's penis once.* I couldn't wait to tell my roommates.

However, as excited as I was about the ding-dong situation, it occurred to me that I wasn't wearing anything that could be remotely considered sexy underwear. I only owned high-cut full-coverage briefs in dark colors. I'm pretty sure sumo wrestlers had sexier underwear than me. See, here's the thing: I have a flat ass, no hips, and a bit of a tummy. Anything other than medical-grade elastic secured around my natural waistline would flop straight to the floor otherwise. And, it's not a sexy panty flop; it's more like the way salsa drops off a tortilla chip onto a carpet.

As Tommy tugged at my jeans, I tried to quickly fashion my unfashionable panties into a makeshift bikini cut by pushing the elastic waistband down closer to my hips. Now it looked like I was wearing an exceptionally baggy bikini brief, which, I reasoned, was better than looking like I was wearing the bottom half of a 1920s-era swimsuit.

We stayed up all night kissing and talking. He had a sharp

sense of humor. But, more important, he was attracted to me! Just by that fact alone, I had to consider him as a contender. Maybe I could learn to love his beer belly. It wasn't that bad. I'm sure it'd make a nice pillow or something. He said he adored my long legs and my green eyes and my soft skin. I was like, "This skin? It's all right, I guess."

"Don't do that," he snapped.

"Do what?"

"Try to talk me out of liking you. You can't do it. It won't happen. Did anyone ever tell you that you talk too much?"

"Ha! I guess I do."

"No, I'm *telling* you that you do. Just relax. I'm not going anywhere."

And I believed him.

He watched me get dressed in the morning with a big, goofy grin slapped on his face. He really seemed to be enjoying himself with me. I, however, was a nervous wreck. My brain was on overdrive trying to figure out a million things simultaneously: Are we dating now? Are we official? Do I want to date him? Am I attracted to him? What would my family think of him? What would my friends think of him? Where is this going? Do I have time to fall in love? Am I ready to fall in love? Could I fall in love with him?

"What's wrong?" He sat up in bed, the sheets loose around his waist. "Stop pacing around. C'mere." I sat down about a foot away from him on the bed, but he wound his arms around my waist and pulled me closer. "Have I told you how beautiful you are today yet?"

"Only about a million times."

"Because you are." I blushed at that. "All right. Let's get brunch. I'm taking you out." We strolled over to Tom's Restaurant on 112th Street because he recognized the place from *Seinfeld*. He said that he'd always wanted to go. We held hands as we walked to the subway. When we parted ways, he promised to call me soon. I had learned nothing from my fling with Wyatt: In my mind, Tommy and I were now in a serious, committed relationship. He called two days later and asked me out to dinner. I had homework to do, but seeing Tommy sounded like more fun so I agreed to meet him.

He took me to Kate's Joint, a vegan restaurant tucked away on the Lower East Side. We split an order of sweet potato fries and giggled a lot. I didn't hesitate when he asked me to go back to his place in Brooklyn. I followed his lead as we navigated our way back to his neighborhood. We stepped over two syringes, a crackhead, and a used condom on the way back to his house. It was like a greatest hits compilation of all the things Barnard's pamphlets had warned me about.

His apartment was nestled in the bottom of an old factory building. He had to open four separate doors to access it. It was nice, I guess, if you're into dungeons.

Of course the first things that caught my eye as soon as we stepped into his apartment were two of those wavy mirrors you get at IKEA hung up in his wall. God, I hate those mirrors. They're like a shiny tribute to cooked bacon. I can't believe these mirrors are so popular! They're in so many guys' living rooms. I don't know why. I wanted to chuck them to the curb.

"I'm actually pretty wiped out. Mind if we hit the hay?" he asked.

"That's fine with me." I fell asleep wrapped up in his heavily tattooed arms. Everything seemed to be going great. It was his idea to introduce me to his friends and thought that his house party the next week was the perfect time to do it.

"I want to show you off. Come! It'll be so much fun."

"All right," I agreed, warming up to the idea.

But when the party rolled around, I was stressed out beyond belief. This being our third date, I knew from my extensive men's magazine reading that this was a make-or-break evening. I had read an article in *Details* that basically said, and I'm paraphrasing, that most men expect a woman to put out by the third date. If she doesn't, then she's a frigid dud who should be immediately dumped. I'm not kidding. This seemed to be a universal expectation. I assumed that this was the night Tommy was going to make his move and seal the deal with me, and I wasn't sure if I was ready. I volleyed it around in my brain all day. Should I put out to keep him around? Should I hold out until I was sure that I really loved him? How would I know that I loved him unless he stuck around? I was so nervous on the subway that I almost puked twice.

The party was great. I met all of his friends, an eclectic mix of musicians and artists. Tommy got drunk and seemed to get increasingly irritated that I wouldn't "just have a beer."

"You knew I didn't drink when you met me," I deadpanned, matching his irritation level that he wouldn't drop the issue.

"I thought I would've broken you from that habit by now. I

usually do it right away. At least, that's how it's happened with other girls. They always start out going, 'wah wah, I don't drink,' but after spending time with me, they wise up. Before you know it, they're full-on lushes." I got very quiet after he said that. I crossed my arms.

"Oh, come on! You know I'm only playing around. Relax! Have a beer! Oh, wait. You don't do that. I keep forgetting. See? This is so hard!"

The *other girls*. Right. As if I weren't self-conscious enough about my lack of experience with men, he had to go throw it in my face about how much more action he'd had than me. I was deflated. I would've left right then, but I was in deep Brooklyn and I wasn't even sure how to get back to the subway from his place. Plus, it was pretty late and I really didn't want to walk around by myself in a neighborhood with syringes lying around like roadkill. I figured the safest thing to do was to wait to leave in the morning in the daylight. I had trouble maintaining eye contact with him, though, and retreated to the living room to make small talk with Stan, a graffiti artist with paint-splattered sneakers.

Everyone left around three A.M., and we finally went to bed. He started going at it with me, and I froze up like a Popsicle. I deflected his advances like a hockey goalie. I didn't think I was ready to take it any further with him. So when he started fumbling with my bra, I panicked and pushed him away.

"Anna, what's wrong?"

"I'm not sure if I'm ready for this." I had buckled under the third-date rule.

"Ready for what? What are you talking about? We're just having fun."

"I don't know how to tell you this, but I'm waiting until marriage."

"You're *what*?"

"Marriage. I'm waiting until marriage to have sex. I wasn't sure how to tell—" As soon as the word *marriage* rolled off my tongue, I wanted to scoop it back in. But I couldn't. And I'm pretty sure he heard it, because he made this face at me that looked like he was wearing the mask from *Scream*.

He let out a loud groan, then rolled over. I tried to wind my arm around his waist, but he pushed it off. Here's the thing: I wasn't waiting until marriage to have sex. I have *no idea* why I said that. And I couldn't take it back; it was already said. What I meant to say was that I wasn't ready at *that moment* because I didn't know if I was in love with him, and that comment about the other girls he'd been with made me feel unspecial, and I thought we should take it a bit slower and *Details* magazine said that tonight we'd have to do it so I felt pressured by the men's magazine industry to put out, but somehow those words didn't come out of my mouth. You want to know what bums a twenty-six-year-old guy out while he's trying to get his swerve on? Blurt out the word *marriage*. It's a total boner-killer.

The next day when we woke up, he barely spoke to me. I wanted to cry, which isn't a good look for the morning after spending the night with a guy. He didn't even walk me fully to the subway; he just pointed in the general direction and said, "Take a right after two blocks. You'll see it." He didn't even kiss me good-bye. We were totally over. Talk about a walk of shame, right? I was walkin' that walk for sure.

The forty-five-minute train ride back to my place was a nightmare. I was alone with my regret, reliving the night over and over in my head. How do you tell someone that you aren't waiting until marriage even though you said that you were? Did I ruin things between us? Was something wrong with me? I didn't have the skills to make the situation better. I wouldn't even know where to start. Fuck it.

When I got home, I canceled my subscription to *Details* magazine. I'm not good at being a male fantasy. I'm just Anna, a super-tall, full-coverage brief-wearing, supportive sneaker-sporting spazz who has no idea how to conduct herself around the opposite sex.

# CHAPTER 6

## Halloweenies

I used to love Halloween when I was younger, but I think that it wasn't so much that I loved the holiday as much as I just loved having access to free candy. Add candy to any holiday and chances are that I'd fully throw my support behind its existence. However, as much as I love free candy, I hate coming up with clever costumes, so that's where Halloween and I don't see eye to eye.

I'm jealous of people who can come up with awesome costumes because it's a skill that's eluded me my entire life. Believe me, if I could pop a pill to suddenly knock out killer costumes, I'd do it in a heartbeat. But until the pharmaceutical companies make the development of costume-enhancing drugs a priority, I'm out of luck.

I don't think my aversion to Halloween costumes is genetic because my younger sister, Rachel, is a costume genius. She's the Michael Jordan of Halloween costumes. She's so good at it that she should really list it on her résumé in the "other skills" section. Hell, she should teach a seminar on it at the local community college learning annex: *That's* how good she is.

Every year she puts together a timely, interesting costume. Frankly, it's annoying. One Halloween, she nailed it as Snow White, wearing the perfect Snow White dress with red puffed sleeves and her hair styled into a perfect, bouncy bob. She looked fantastic. My costume, on the other hand, was not only forgettable, but also downright stupid. I wore dark jeans and a black T-shirt and told people that I was an NYU student. Can it get much lazier than that? It's one step above not wearing a costume at all.

The next year, she knocked it out of the park as Wonder Woman. She even had a gold lasso and gold wrist cuffs that took her costume to the next level. That year, I tossed on a flannel shirt that I found under my bed, didn't brush my hair, and told people that I was an extra in the movie *Singles*. Are you getting the picture?

The following year, she blew people's hair back with her Luigi from Mario Bros. costume. If anyone could rock a fake mustache and make it look pretty, it's Rachel. People were taking photos with her at every party she attended. She probably got tagged in at least five great Facebook pics that night. She plans her costume months in advance and makes sure to swing by several Halloween parties to show it off to as many people as possible. I am the exact opposite of her in this regard: I'm indifferent. I've never shopped for a costume. I've never had a good idea for one. And, every year without fail, I wait until the last possible second to think of a costume idea that requires the minimum amount of creativity required. Preferably, I'd like to already own all the required materials and not invest more than ten minutes putting the damn thing together.

I'll stand in front of my closet with my hands on my hips, scanning my clothes and hoping inspiration strikes. "What's this, a black turtleneck? Fine, I'll be a beatnik. Halloween: *done.*" Consequently, I was a beatnik for every Halloween four years in a row.

It wasn't until I moved to Philadelphia that I began to make more of an effort, costumewise. I had been living in New York for close to six years and was feeling restless, so when my parents announced that they were moving to South Jersey, I decided to move twenty-five minutes away to Philly.

The only person I knew here was the singer of a popular punk band named Dylan. I had interviewed him for a zine a few months before and he talked Philly up, gushing about what a fantastic place it was to live. So after I moved here, I went to see his band play at a dingy bar on South Street. That's where I met my soon-to-be best friend, Kat.

Decked out in black pumps, a bright red polka-dot dress, and red lipstick to match, she stood out from the crowd. I was immediately drawn to her. She was totally different from any of my low-key New York friends, who would usually just wear boring jeans and plain T-shirts in neutral colors. Meeting her was like watching television in black-and-white my whole life then finally switching to high-definition color TV.

Kat was a free spirit, ready to grab life by the horns. She was loud, smart, and funny. The first time we hung out, she took me to a sixties soul dance party and we danced so hard that our makeup ran off our faces.

After that, we hit up dance parties all around town, staying out until they flicked on the house lights at two A.M. She introduced me to all of Philly's movers and shakers, musicians, deejays, and scenesters. For the first time in my life, I was finally having fun.

We moved in together into an apartment in the Art Museum Area. She was like a sister from another mister teaching me how to do the kinds of things girls mastered in middle school. She showed me how to curl my hair properly, how to paint my nails and advised me on which dresses flattered my figure best.

And Kat was the one who introduced me to a wonderful thing called whiskey. I did my first shot with her and it quickly became a staple in our home. Thanks to Jack Daniel's, I became a kissing bandit, making out with a buffet of short guys across the city. Her balls-to-the-wall attitude was rubbing off on me. After years of overanalyzing every minuscule interaction I've ever had with a guy, whiskey made me not give a fuck. For a neurotic Jew like me, it was a relief to shut my brain off for a few hours. All my worries melted away.

My friendship with Kat made me realize how sheltered I'd been. Crippled by pamphlet-induced fear for the first half of my twenties, I'd barely lived my life. She seemed light-years ahead of me in so many areas. She had more hangovers, more cocktails, more motorcycle rides, more smashed beer bottles, more broken hearts, more *everything*. If this were Party University, I'd be a freshman and she was most definitely a senior. It made me want to experience as much life as possible, as quickly as possible.

With Kat at my side for my first Philadelphia Halloween, I had to step up my costume game. She was dressed as Axl Rose, complete with a blond wig and fake tattoos she drew on with a Sharpie. I tossed on tan boots and a denim skirt, twisted a red bandanna around my neck, and pulled my hair into pigtails: Voila! I was a cowgirl. Unfortunately, everyone I talked to that night just thought I was a hipster. After two hours, I decided to just go with it and abandoned the cowgirl ruse. Fine, everyone, you win; I'll be a hipster. See? That's how little I care about my costume: I'll abandon the concept in a flash. I wasn't just lazy; I was apathetic, too.

To be honest, I resent feeling like I have to wow everyone with a cool costume every single year. Haven't I earned the right to not care about my Halloween costume yet? When does it end? Hey, I'm just here for the free boxes of Good & Plentys; no need to bring a wacky costume into the mix.

The worst was Halloween 2004, when I went to a huge party in a North Philly warehouse sans costume. I arrived in my normal Friday night outfit of a short dress and black boots, and then I realized that every other person had come up with the most elaborate, clever costumes I'd ever seen. My cheeks burned red with shame. I'd never felt so inadequate before. I couldn't make eye contact with anyone at the party, which turned out to be pretty easy because the costumes I saw were so advanced beyond anything I could ever put together, I couldn't recognize anyone anyway.

Looking around the room, I saw someone dressed as Osama bin Laden wearing a turban made out of spaghetti and meatballs, four girls dressed as Tetris pieces that fit together, a human disco ball, and Crocodile Dundee. I saw Marcia Brady getting down on the dance floor. I could tell it was her because she was wearing a sixties dress with long brown hair parted in the middle and had a tiny football affixed to her nose. She was dancing with Princess Leia and the Queen of England.

Clearly, my Old Navy dress did not make the cut here. I felt like I was chaperoning the party, not elevating it to epic levels of Halloween-ness. I was in over my head! I was among the kinds of Halloween freaks who invest time and money into their costume. There are two kinds people in this world: those who coordinate trips to rural thrift stores to assemble their costumes, and people like me, who just hope that no one gives them shit for not dressing up. I was a different class of citizen, a mark of shame on an otherwise festive holiday.

This was the first time in my life that people looked disappointed that I had attended an event. If I had harnessed the energy from all the eye rolls I received for not wearing a costume, I could've lit up the Vegas strip for a week. I wanted to leave immediately.

The next year, I was determined not to make the same mistake, so for a Halloween party at Johnny Brenda's, a loud, hip bar in Fishtown, I dressed all in black, pressed a handful of baby powder on my face, and went out as a ghoul. Honestly, the only thing ghoulish about me was the ratty black wig I bought that afternoon at a drugstore; it looked like it had crawled onto my head and died a slow, painful death.

I tried to channel Elvira with my look, but between my patchy-looking face and my knotted wig hair, I think I looked more like a crazy cat lady who reeked of litter box turds. However, in the right light, I could probably pass for a villager burned in a volcanic lava explosion, which, I reasoned, was still better than looking like a hipster.

Halfway through the night, I became so irritated with the scratchy wig that I pulled it off altogether, totally breaking the Halloween etiquette code. Sure, my dome felt relief, but my real hair was matted down so severely that I looked even worse, like a homeless suicidal clown. When I got home and saw my reflection in the mirror, well, that was the real fright of the evening. *I hate Halloween costumes!*

Given that, out of everyone on the planet, I'm the worst candidate to take as a date to a Halloween party. But in a bout of costume optimism, I agreed to go with Max to his friend's Halloween shindig. I had met Max a few weeks before and this was our first official hangout. He seemed like an all right guy. He worked at Mugshots, a coffee shop near my apartment, and he had a habit of shaving off fourteen cents so my iced coffee order would come to an even two dollars. I thought that was cool. He was 5'11", which was a bit on the taller side for me, but I wanted to be open to anything. I was working a desk job at Temple University, so my life was pretty boring. Max seemed like a breath of fresh air.

We started talking one day because his band was playing a show the next week. He handed me a flyer and suggested I check them out. They were called Jinx Remover and they were playing the North Star Bar on a Monday night. According to Max, they sounded like a cross between Huey Lewis and the News and Joy Division. I have no idea what that would sound like and I can't tell you because I didn't attend, but it opened up a dialogue between us.

He was handsome in that shaggy, effortless way that all guys who work at a café seem to master: thin thrift store T-shirts, ratty gray corduroy pants, and his curly moptop had perpetual bedhead. His tattoos were stupid and blurry. I knew I should've been turned off by them, but dare I say it, I thought they were cute.

The first time I noticed one peeking out from under the sleeve of his T-shirt, I playfully asked, "What is this?" as I touched it with my finger.

He pushed his sleeve up and said, "It's supposed to be a family crest. I got it done when I was, like, nineteen." He moved his attention over to his other arm. "This one over here? This is my skateboarding crew's insignia. Yes, we had an insignia. Don't laugh. My friends all have it, too. It's kinda stupid."

"It's not stupid!" I protested.

"Yeah, it is. It's totally stupid." He pointed to his forearm. "I got that one when I was, Christ, seventeen, I think? This one over here is a T. rex eating a slice of pizza riding a surfboard.

That one I got on a dare." He chuckled, then rubbed over the skin wistfully.

When he asked me to go to his friend's Halloween party, I agreed partly because I felt bad that I didn't go to his show the week before and partly because I was open to the idea of riding the night with him. Guys who have tattoos of T. rexes eating pizza are usually a fun time, I reasoned. This would also be a chance to redeem myself for the Halloween ghoul fuckup. I resolved to put more effort into my costume this year and was pleased at the chance to do so.

We talked briefly about our costume situation beforehand. He said that he was going to go as the Fonz. I decided to go as a mallpunk, replete with a black Good Charlotte T-shirt, streaked mascara running down my cheeks, and ripped fishnet stockings. I even made a zine to pass out called *The Hot Topic* that had pictures of all of my favorite bands and handwritten lists of things that I loved and things that I hated.

For example, things I loved were Slurpees from 7-Eleven, record stores, and Converse sneakers. Things I hated were my teachers, my parents, and MTV. The centerfold was a crudely photocopied ad for the Vans Warped Tour. I even brought along a few issues of *Alternative Press* to cart around as additional props. Personally, I thought I nailed the costume. As a chronic non-costumer, I was proud of myself. I didn't even need to buy anything except the Good Charlotte shirt, so my costume was economical, too. Score!

The next chilly Saturday night, Max picked me up in his beige Honda. He was dressed in a brown flannel shirt, a puffy brown vest, and old, faded jeans. No slicked-back hair, no leather jacket; if he was the Fonz, it was the worst version of the Fonz I'd ever seen.

"A-o! O-a! Where's the Fonz?" I said in a loose approximation of an Italian accent.

"First, that's Tony Danza in *Who's the Boss* who talks like that, not the Fonz. The Fonz just says, 'Aaaaaay' whilst giving a thumbs-up. Secondly, there's been a change of plans: I'm going as Dan Connor."

I frowned. "The little kid in *The Terminator*? Dude, he wore a Public Enemy shirt." I motioned toward his outfit. "You're way off."

"No, Dan Connor aka Roseanne's husband on the show *Roseanne* aka America's favorite middle-class suburban dad of the nineties. You know, John Goodman's character. Now you see it, right?" He smiled, nodding. I squinted, sizing him up.

"But you're not even fat."

"I have curly hair. Can't deny that."

"Yeah, I don't see it. From where I'm sitting, you just look like a cool guy who works at a coffee shop. I could maybe give you Seth Rogen circa *Freaks and Geeks*. Maybe."

"That's 'cause I'm not talking about drywall while pounding back cans of cheap beer. You'll see when we get there. My costume will be a hit."

"All right, whatever you say."

"What's your costume again?" he asked.

"A mallpunk! Check out this Good Charlotte shirt. I even made a zine. See?" I tossed an issue of *The Hot Topic* at him.

He looked at the cover briefly and then tossed it in the backseat like it was a flyer for fifty percent off a Brazilian bikini wax: something that he immediately sensed he'd have no use for.

"A mallpunk, huh? You look like a Goth kid."

"I'm not Gothy. I'm punky," I clarified.

"Whatever. Let's do this. You ready to go?"

"I'm totally ready."

"Sweet."

As we pulled out onto the street, I looked around his chariot and noticed that he had this long chain dangling from his rearview mirror. It looked like a beaded lanyard that an old woman would use to hang her reading glasses from, and it was hard to ignore it because it kept banging against the dashboard at every turn he made.

I'm sorry, did he mug Zoltar and is showcasing this chain as a trophy? Did he swipe it from Janet Jackson's face in the "Runaway" video? If he *had* to drape something over his rearview mirror, I could maybe understand an air freshener. I'd even understand if he hung a pair of fuzzy dice in a retro way. I could kinda see it if he were an old-school rockabilly guy with a bitchin' vintage car. But his beige Honda was about as edgy as Play-Doh. Seriously, but there was no need for car jewelry here. It was like his mirror had a belly chain or like his car got its eyebrow pierced in 1997 and still wears the thing because it thinks it's cool. His car was basically Fergie from Black Eyed Peas.

"So, what kind of girls do you normally date?" I asked. I had decided that I wasn't attracted to him, so I was just making conversation.

He smiled and leaned toward me, like he was about to tell me a secret. "I gotta be honest with you: I like crazy girls." He stopped to gauge my reaction. I didn't have one. I blinked. Was this guy for real? He kept going.

"You know, the ones that are a bit unstable, like they might threaten to stab you with a pair of rusty scissors when you don't answer their texts or some shit." That description was a little too specific, which made me think that he had actually dated a girl who did that. And he was into it!

"What can I say? It keeps things interesting, ya know?" He grinned and shrugged his shoulders like the whole thing was out of his control.

News flash: I am not the kind of girl to do that. At all. Ever. Frankly, I'm more of a Girl, Continued than a Girl, Interrupted. I didn't say anything after that. I just sat in the car and looked at the South Philly scenery, which mostly consisted of cracked sidewalks and trash blowing around the street like tumbleweeds. Yeah, I was definitely not interested in him anymore.

We parked outside a dark brick building with a few people standing outside smoking cigarettes. "Oh. Are we here?"

"Nope. Beer run. Wanna come in?"

"Sure."

I followed him into the Pope, a dive bar on the corner of Tenth Street and Passyunk Avenue. Led Zeppelin was blasting over the jukebox as everyone sat at the bar, sipping their pints.

"Hey!" The bartender nodded at us.

"Hey! Can I get a six-pack of Kenzingers to go?" Max asked.

"Yup. That'll be thirteen dollars."

Max reached into his pocket and produced a wad of crumpled dollar bills to pay for it. His money looked like little dented Ping-Pong balls. What, was he against folding? Those are some crinkled money balls, my man.

We secured the beer in a brown paper bag, hopped back into his car, and drove the ten blocks to the party. It was tricky finding street parking, and we ended up having to park two blocks away. As we briskly walked on the chilly South Philly streets, I asked, "Whose party is this again?"

"Daisy and Chuck's."

"Oh, okay. I have no idea who they are."

"Hurry up! The light's turning yellow. Come on!" He started to run into the street.

I teetered on the edge of the curb, assessing my chances of making it before the light turned red.

"We can totally make it. Hurry up!" he yelled, clutching the six-pack of beer to his chest.

"Ahhhhhhhhhhhh!" I jogged to catch up with him. I have no idea why I did that. When did this evening turn into the obstacle course on *Double Dare*? Do I have to find a flag up a huge nostril next? Maybe catch a rubber chicken in a basket affixed to my head? When I agreed to go out with him tonight, I didn't expect to find myself in my own, personal live version of Frogger. The chunky boots I wore as part of my costume were definitely not made for sprinting. I kept screaming, trying to catch up to him.

As I was running through the street, I thought about why I

didn't just wait on the curb and let him risk his life darting into traffic. It's what I should've done. Someone honked at me, which made me scream louder. I was going to kill Max if I ever made it across the street alive.

Well, you will be pleased to know that we both made it across the street alive and I didn't kill him. Instead of murdering Max, we found the party and walked right in. Right off the bat, everyone there had the best costumes I'd ever seen in my life. Someone was dressed like Iron Man. A girl was dressed like Jackie O and another was dressed like Cher, licking her lips and flinging her long black hair off her shoulders. Abraham Lincoln and Indiana Jones were fiddling with the stereo while Bill Cosby and Bruce Lee sat on the couch catching up.

Daisy, dressed as a mermaid, walked over to greet us.

"Max!" She embraced him. "Thanks so much for coming. And who are you supposed to be?"

"I'm Dan Connor, you know, from *Roseanne*."

"Ha! I love it!" she exclaimed. "Oh, that's hilarious. Dan Connor. I can't say we have any other Dan Connors here tonight." She leaned in toward us and whispered, "We already have three Batmans; can you believe it? Wait, Batmen. I don't know which one is the proper word. I'll go with Batmen. We have a gaggle of Batmen." She turned her attention to me. "And you are?"

"Hi! My name is Anna and I'm a mallpunk," I blurted out. "I even made my own zine. See?" I held up the dozen copies of *The Hot Topic* and shoved one at her. She took it, looked at me like I had just given her a pamphlet about detecting the early stages of syphilis, and quickly flipped it under her arm.

"Well, I'm happy you two are here. Come on in. The kitchen is straight back. Chuck made some spooky punch, so feel free to help yourselves. Oh, Max, you brought beer! Fantastic. I'll take that." As she scooped up the beer, Max went over to talk to a buddy and I retreated to the kitchen.

The spooky punch was exactly what I'd imagined: a mixture of various cheap liquors and some kind of orange drink swirled together in a giant crystal punch bowl. A huge block of sherbet sat in the middle, slowly melting. Let me tell you, that spooky punch was strong as hell. It was so strong, I winced a bit as I took a sip.

It was then that I laid my eyes on the hottest man I'd ever seen (that day), sitting next to a dish filled with candy corn. He was dressed as FDR with a blue suit, a red tie, silver wire-framed glasses, and—the kicker—he was seated in a wheelchair with a red plaid blanket draped over his legs like he was ready for an impromptu fireside chat. His wispy blond hair was combed down like Bart Simpson on class picture day and I have to say, he looked exceedingly presidential situated in the middle of a crowded kitchen in a South Philly house party. I forgot all about Max; I was too focused on this mystery man. I was captivated.

Here's the thing: I couldn't tell if the wheelchair was part of the costume or if he really used a wheelchair. I wasn't even sure how I'd go about finding out. How do you find out something like that? The blanket was covering his legs, so I couldn't see if his legs were in braces or not. Do I ask him if he can't walk? How would I ask? What's the standard here? Should I knock the wheelchair over and see if he crawls back in or stands up? I wasn't prepared for this.

For the sake of argument, I assumed that he really was a wheelchair user. I'd never dated a dude in a wheelchair before. I considered what it would be like. Frankly, it seemed kinda cool. I'd happily wheel his adorable face around town. I'd give him sponge baths and tie his sneakers. I'd load him into my car and let him sit in the aisle when we went out to the movies. Sign me the fuck up.

I sipped my punch as I watched him roll around the kitchen, assessing my chances. He wasn't wearing a wedding ring, so that was a good sign. Maybe he was available. God, I hoped he was available. I needed a good, original pickup line if I was going to say hi. I practiced a few in my head:

"Hi! Man, you are, like, the spitting image of FDR." That was too clunky.

"Hey! You roll here often?" Ouch. That was probably offensive.

"I like your blanket. Is that a wool blend?" Oh God, that was even worse. What am I, Martha Stewart? (Now that I think about it, that would've been a good costume.)

"Hi! My name is Anna." Ding ding ding, we have a winner. It was the least psycho-sounding line of the bunch and I couldn't think of anything else. It was the winner by default.

With my pickup line settled on, I marched right up to him

and plunged my hand in the candy dish behind him because I chickened out at the last minute. I'm usually not shy about meeting guys, but this was a little trickier for some reason. I got flustered! I never really get nervous around guys and here I was sweating bullets.

Since I didn't have the nerve to say anything just yet, I hovered behind him, stuffing candy corn in my pockets like a creepy uncle. That was when I realized that his handsome face came up to my thigh. It was hard enough talking to short guys who are at boob level, but thigh level? I needed a manual for how to proceed. Could it be done? Could I have a relationship with a guy whose sight line came to a few inches below my crotch? This was uncharted territory for me.

I gulped down my spooky punch and headed back to the punch bowl on the counter for a refill. Max appeared beside me.

"You having fun?"

"Oh yeah. Totally. This is a great party. You?"

"Fuck yes. Check this out." He popped open a beer can and chugged the entire thing in five loud gulps.

"Wow. That's impressive," I deadpanned.

"Dude, WWDCD!"

"And what does that mean?"

"What Would Dan Connor Do is what that means," Max asserted.

"Oh, I see. So I assume Dan Connor would chug a beer. And talk about drywall construction. Don't forget that part."

"I'm gonna grab another beer. Need anything?"

"Nah, I'm good. I'm sticking with the spooky punch."

Max dug his head in the fridge looking for a new brew while I resumed staring at FDR. After Max found another can, he raised it toward me, nodded, and walked into the living room. I was ready to make my move on our former president.

I knelt down beside him to introduce myself. We were at eye level now and he seemed startled because I basically appeared out of nowhere.

"You know, I can honestly say that you have the best costume here tonight." He stared at me blankly. I puttered on, "My name is Anna. I don't believe we've met. What's your name?" Before he could answer my question, a problem immediately presented itself: I didn't stretch before I decided to squat down beside him. As it turned out, my legs were not interested in bending down like that. My knees seized up and started to hurt immediately. I ignored the pain as I listened for his response.

But before he told me what his name was, I had a thought: I hope it's something Roosevelt-y, preferably Franklin or Teddy. That would be a best-case scenario here. I tried not to hide my disappointment when he said his name was Bobby.

*Hmmmm. Wait, there's a Bobby Kennedy! That's political. I could work with that.*

"Hi, Bobby. Nice to meet you. I really like your costume."

"Okay. Thanks. Yeah, you just said that."

I cleared my throat. "Do you like mine?" I leaned back a bit so he could take it all in.

"What are you, a Goth, uh, person?"

"No, silly. I'm a mallpunk! See? That's why I'm carrying

these around." I hoisted up my magazines. "It's *Alternative Press*, the leading magazine for mallpunkers. You know, it goes with the costume." I pointed to my chest. "And I'm wearing this Good Charlotte shirt. That's part of the costume, too."

He shrugged. Apparently, he was unfamiliar with every single thing I was both talking about and wearing.

"Didn't you come here with Max?"

"Oh! You know him?"

"Yeah, I've met him once before. He's a nice guy."

"Max and I are just friends. Ha! We're not together or anything. Oh, nothing like that." I tried my best to explain to him that despite the male companion I arrived with, I was in fact available. Very available. Apparently, I don't know how to do this without sounding like I'm clinically insane. I barfed out an entire paragraph in an attempt to clarify the situation.

"Max? He's my homeboy. I mean my homie. My *friend*. That's what I meant to say. He's just a friend. A buddy. Seriously, there's *nothing* going on between us. He's definitely no one I'd consider sleeping with. And I haven't! Oh, God no. Really, there's *nothing* here. He's actually repulsive to me. There's no way I'd date him. Also, he has this weird habit of smelling like soup all the time. Like a pungent, hearty lentil soup, which is just yuck! So, you know. Yeah. No."

I didn't have anything to say to him after that. And it got awkward pretty quickly squatting on the kitchen floor in the middle of a raging house party trying to make lighthearted small talk while balancing my red Solo cup on the arm of his wheelchair.

Besides, the shooting pains in my legs were too intense to ignore. I tried my best not to show my stinging discomfort. "Well, it was nice talking with you, Bobby." I leaned on his chair as I pulled myself up, like a creaky old man with arthritis hoisting himself off a La-Z-Boy recliner. I even made the kind of noise old people make when they get up off a low couch, a deep "ugh" kind of noise. I don't think he found it hot.

Not knowing what else to do, I searched the party for Daisy to do a little background research.

I found her upstairs by the bathroom.

"Oh, Daisy! Just the girl I'm looking for. I have a question."

"Yeah?"

I took her elbow and whispered, "It's private."

She looked panicked. "All right."

"FDR. Downstairs. What's his deal?" She seemed relieved that it was only an inquiry about another guest, not a confession that I'd killed someone and hidden the body in her backyard.

I caught sight of Max on the stairwell. He cracked open a beer can and again nodded while he raised it in my direction. He mouthed the word *drywall*, then slammed the beer, letting out a loud belch that probably registered on the low end of the Richter scale.

"Oh, the guy in the suit? That's Bobby. He's so cool, right?"

"Yeah, he's great. Is he available? I mean, is he single?" I tried not to sound too eager, but it was totally obvious that I was eager.

"Unfortunately, no. In fact, he's engaged to Kirsten, the girl in the corner dressed like a princess over there. They're moving to Boston next month."

"Oh." I attempted to hide my disappointment, but thanks to the spooky punch, my acting skills were suffering. I didn't even ask if he was really in a wheelchair or if it was part of his costume. Either way, the dream was dead.

"You're interested in Bobby? I thought you were here with Max," Daisy asked.

"Oh, I am. We're just friends. I think. This is actually our first date. Hangout! I mean hangout."

"Really!" Her eyes grew wide. "How's it going so far?"

"Um, it's okay." We both craned our necks to see Max running in a circle in the living room, high-fiving everyone. "He seems like the life of the party."

Her voice lowered. "Have you met Darryl yet?"

"There's someone here dressed like Daryl Hall? That's so cool. Which one is he?"

"No, *Darryl.* You haven't, have you? You'll see what I mean. Trust me." She looked at Max, and then looked back to me. "You will definitely meet Darryl tonight."

"All right, whatever you say. I'm going to grab some more of this spooky punch. This shit is delicious."

I knocked back my third helping of spooky punch and took a seat on the couch. Bobby was wheeling himself around like a cutie pie. Max was trying to stage a stereo takeover, loudly insisting that "What this party really needs is some motherfuckin' AC/DC! Am I right or am I right?"

I turned to the guy next to me.

"Hey. Happy Halloween."

"Oh, yeah. Happy Halloween and whatnot." We clinked red Solo cups.

"I like your costume." I looked at his long beard and quipped, "What are you, ZZ Top?"

"Ha. Yes! You guessed it."

We sat in silence for a minute before he said, "Wanna go upstairs and make out?"

I thought about it: I was bored. Max was ignoring me because I didn't come in a twelve-ounce can with a pull tab. Bobby was adorable and engaged. I drained the last of the spooky punch in my cup before I said, "Sure."

We found an empty bedroom upstairs and immediately started going at it. A fat, orange tabby cat sat on the bed, staring at me like it was saying, *Really, Anna? This guy?* I kept making eye contact with the feline by accident, which freaked me out. I halted things after a few minutes to find out a little more about this guy's situation.

"So, what's your name?"

"Blanket."

"Blanket? Like Michael Jackson's kid?"

"Nah, I'm just messing with you. It's Arnold."

"Arnold? Really?"

"Nah. I'm just fucking around. My name is Donnie." I stared at him. "No, really, it's Donnie."

"Hi, Donnie. Do you like my costume?"

He looked me up and down. "What are you, Helena Bonham Carter?"

"No, I'm a mallpunk. I made my own zine and everything."

"Cool." For the fourth time that night, someone didn't look at my stupid zine. I tossed the rest of them toward a trash can in the corner along with my copies of *Alternative Press*. I'd lasted exactly one hour at a Halloween party before abandoning a crucial element of my costume. That was probably a new record for me.

Donnie didn't ask what my name was, which was fine. In fact, it felt exhilarating. Even as we were kissing, I knew I'd probably never see him again. He was disposable, like a pink plastic razor. Speaking of razors, his beard was long and burly. It touched the top of his chest.

As we started kissing some more, someone started banging on the door.

"Donnie, you asshole! Are you in there?"

"I think someone's looking for you." I said, pulling away from his embrace.

"Oh, yeah. That's probably my wife."

"Your *wife*?"

"Yeah."

"You didn't tell me you were married!"

"You didn't ask!"

Technically, he was right. I did not ask. I didn't realize that it was my responsibility to suss out his relationship status. My random hookup fantasy dissolved and I realized instead of making out with a semi-hot stranger, I was messing around with a married man. Obviously, I was repulsed and looked at him like his face had just turned into a pile of slugs.

I opened the door and saw a short girl dressed as Cleopatra standing there.

"What the hell?" she yelled at me.

"Dude, he's all yours."

She didn't waste her time with me, but bolted into the room with a trail of obscenities flying out of her mouth. It was time to leave.

I went downstairs to find Max passed out on the sofa.

"Hey, Max. You ready to go?" I poked his arm, bringing him back to consciousness.

"My name's not Max. There is no Max because Darryl's in the house, *motherfuckers!*"

Ah! Darryl is Max's drunk alter ego. For those unfamiliar with the concept, this is when a dude undergoes a personality transformation when he gets hammered and decides to assign a name to the other drunker, wilder side of him; a Mr. Hyde to his Dr. Jekyll, if you will. For some reason, guys always give their other halves manly names, like Derek, Biff, Marco, or Steve.

"Darryl is officially *here*, you assholes," he said to the room, louder. He kicked over an empty beer can on the coffee table for emphasis.

"Come on. Let's go, Max." I slid my arm under him and hoisted him up, but he pushed me off him.

"Don't try and act all nice now."

"What do you mean?"

"I saw you go upstairs with that scumbag Donnie. And Daisy told me you've been eyebanging FDR all night."

"I was just trying to have some fun," I tried to explain but Max waved me off with his hand.

"I already told you, my name's not Max. It's Darryl. Get it right!"

"Okay, Darryl. Listen, I'm sorry. I didn't mean to bum you out."

"You didn't even come to see my band play," he whimpered. "That hurt my feelings!"

Well, now I felt terrible.

"C'mon, Darryl. Let me drive you home."

"You're a very mean lady."

"I'm not a mean lady. I'm impulsive and I have a thing for wheelchair-bound ex-presidents, but I'm not mean. Where are your keys?"

He dug into his pocket and handed them over, then looked at me quizzically.

"Where are your zines? Didn't you have, like, an entire stack of them?"

"They're in zine heaven now," I said, shuffling toward the front door.

"Oh. Sorry 'bout what I said earlier. Darryl got out of his cage tonight."

"That's okay."

"I don't think you're mean."

"Thanks, buddy. You know how you like crazy girls? I guess I like weird guys."

"So if I had a long-ass beard or a wheelchair you'd be into me?"

"And if you were shorter. Short and weird is basically my wheelhouse."

As we walked outside into the crisp October air, I turned around and saw Bobby smoking a cigarette on the steps. I thought about pushing Max/Darryl into some nearby bushes to flirt with Bobby some more, but decided against it because that actually would be mean, and I didn't want to have to fish him out of some bushes. There might be thorns.

"Good night, Bobby. It was nice to meet you," I semi-yelled in his direction.

"Yeah! Likewise." With that, he stubbed the butt of his cigarette out and flicked it toward the street. Then, to my amazement, he crawled up the stairs to the top step, where he maneuvered himself back into his chair. Bobby really did use a wheelchair! Then it occurred to me: Maybe he had such a great costume because he's FDR every year. I mean, how many options does he have being in a wheelchair, you know?

I hope that princess Kristin knew how lucky she was, snagging the cutest guy ever. I looked at Max in all of his slurring, droopy-eyed glory and sighed. Someday he was going to make some crazy girl out there a very happy woman.

## CHAPTER 7

# Best Man Bingo

There's something about being surrounded by fancy dresses, fresh flowers, and assigned table seating that turns me into a girl gone wild. Put me in front of an open bar with a crowd of polite acquaintances and I'll pretty much act like I'm on spring break at Daytona Beach in 1987 for the entire affair.

I love going to weddings because that's when I really let loose. When I say that I let loose, I don't just pull off my eyeglasses and take out my ponytail like how secretly sexy lady nerds do it in the movies. I unleash my inner Courtney Love on the place.

For example, anyone involved directly or peripherally with the wedding is fair game to hit on. I will smooch anything not bolted down to the floor. Distant cousins, waitstaff, limo drivers: Everyone has a shot at kissing these lips. I'm probably never going to see any of these guys again so it's totally cool to act as if I'm at a frat party.

Like the figurines planted on top of the wedding cake, hooking up with the best man is on the top tier of wedding traditions. But it takes a set of specific conditions to make landing a best man happen. He's a rare bird! After all, there aren't that many of them at the party. He's a bald eagle, a slot machine jackpot, and the *Amazing Race*'s Travelocity gnome all wrapped into one. Luck, chemistry, hard work, and timing are all factors in landing him.

What's the appeal of bagging a best man? Here's the thing: It's pretty exciting to make out with a moderately hot dude in a tux. It's like being in a James Bond movie or getting felt up by a waiter at a four-star restaurant. What girl could turn that down?

To an outsider watching me swing on a chandelier in a jersey dress from T.J.Maxx's clearance rack, it may not look like I have a lot of rules I observe at weddings. And while there aren't many rules I obey in my day-to-day life, when it comes to weddings, I follow a strict code of behavior. Here are some dos and don'ts I've cobbled together:

> I *DO* make it a point to kick up my heels to all the corny songs that the deejay spins. I'll twirl around the dance floor like a little girl who just got her favorite Barbie doll for her sixth birthday. I'll boogie to "Mambo #5," "The Macarena," and Kool and the Gang's "Celebrate" in a heartbeat. I'll bop

around to the "Electric Slide." I'll shimmy to "Livin' la Vida Loca." Fuck it, after a few glasses of chardonnay, I'll even do the "Y.M.C.A." This is no time for snobbery because snobbery won't get me any action.

I *DO* attend friends' weddings solo. At first, it seems like a daunting prospect to walk in by myself, but I realize that if anything, I'll meet more people because I won't be tethered to a boring date. I'll chat up everyone I meet so by the time the whole affair is over, I'll have, like, five new random Facebook friends, guaranteed.

I *DO* go back to the buffet table for thirds. I've already fit into the dress I'm wearing. Mission accomplished! I've cleared that hurdle so, yes, I'll have another piece of cake, thanks for asking. Besides, fitting into my clothes tomorrow is Future Anna's problem, not Present Anna's. (I really run with the wolves on this one.)

Okay, so I'm dancing to Kool and the Gang by myself, winking at the waitstaff and eyebanging the best man by the chocolate fountain. Sweet. But, I won't get too carried away because there are still some potential pitfalls that I need to avoid.

I *DON'T* flash my boobs to the camera. Yes, it'll seem funny four dirty martinis in, but once the wedding couple has their proofs developed, I'll just make the bride and groom cringe for even inviting me. I speak from experience on this one, guys. My sister Sarah is still pissed at me for my unfortunate nip slip at her wedding. Whoops!

While I'm all for dancing, I *DON'T* dirty dance with a member of either the bride or groom's family because I'll never live it down. I'm still being razzed about grinding on my friend's cousin during her sister's wedding in 2003. Like the 9/11 eagle with a tear running down its eye, her family will never let me forget it.

I *DON'T* hit on the groom before the wedding. And I don't tell him that he would be a better match with me and that his bride always seemed kinda bitchy. Really, I should write this one down on my hand.

Lastly, I *DON'T* pass out on the lawn outside the reception hall. Sure, the cool grass will feel refreshing against my flushed cheeks, but grass stains are never a good look at a formal affair. That's some Long Duk Dong shit right there. Take it from me, you will never know true humiliation until you've been dragged out of a bush totally wasted and subsequently hoisted into the backseat of your parents' Audi at your other sister's wedding.

And, to add insult to drunken injury, thanks to those pesky branches, my hot pink strapless dress was several inches lower than where it should've been according to the picture on the manufacturer's website. Being sharked by shrubbery was a low point in my life. Even Paris Hilton has more class than that.

Follow my lead and you'll be doing so much schmoozin' and boozin' that you won't even remember how you can barely nail down a second date while your peers are lockin' in their soul mates. Oh, that sounds depressing. Well, at least I don't have to write a pile of thank-you cards like they do.

I almost forgot! One more thing:

> I *DO* cheer on any people who attempt to execute the worm in the middle of the dance floor. I'll stand in a loose semicircle with the rest of the party guests, clapping and cheering on this breakdancing one-man entertainment center. He's bringing a little bit of street to the ballroom, which rules. I'll make sure to show him how truly delighted I am at his impromptu performance. I'll hoot and holler like I'm in the audience at *The Arsenio Hall Show* because that is how I appreciate most works of fine art.

My favorite wedding of all time was my college buddy Oliver's wedding a few years ago as it was a chance to reconnect with my old classmates. We'd been out of college for six years at the time of his wedding, which was enough time to get jobs and lose them. We'd all had serious relationships and fucked them up, too. That's the cool thing about being twenty-eight: After you've weathered a few of life's storms, you pretty much know who you are by this age.

At twenty-eight, you're not fully aware of everything about yourself just yet. I'd reckon that I knew myself about eighty-five percent of the way by twenty-eight. For the most part, I knew my habits, tastes, and values. I knew that I will probably never willingly purchase a Limp Bizkit album or attend a church service where people dance around with poisonous snakes. I knew that I would probably never develop a cigar habit or wear a cape in public. I also knew that I probably would never learn how to play the harp or join a street gang in South Central L.A. In fact, I'd put money on it.

However, there was still a bit about myself that I hadn't discovered yet. For instance, I had no idea what kind of parent I'll be. Even though the idea seems far-fetched, I had no idea if I'd ever buy a minivan or purchase massage oils in a concerted effort to "spice up" my love life. I also had no idea what kind of guy I'd even want to settle down with and maybe use those massage oils on. What would he look like? What would he sound like? Who knows? As Tom Petty sang in the song with Johnny Depp in the video, "The future was wide open."

Oliver was my friend Ricky's roommate in my sophomore year of college. He was tall, blond, and skinny, and all the girls got weak knees around him because he was so effortlessly handsome. The fact that he was in a rotating roster of indie rock bands just added to his appeal. I, however, was immune to his charms because tall, lanky blonds did nothing for me. This allowed our friendship to flourish.

My favorite memory of Oliver was when he was getting ready to go out one night and I popped into his room while he assembled his outfit. In total emo style, he was wearing periwinkle shorts, a green striped T-shirt, and black-rimmed glasses that complemented his black Chuck Taylors. He asked me what I thought of his ensemble. I narrowed my eyes and said, "Well, Oliver, you look like a developmentally challenged second grader." He nearly popped a button laughing so hard. We still crack up about that.

Oliver was marrying Katya, an absolute darling. She had long, straight brown hair and glowy skin, like she washed her face with fairies' eyelashes and ground unicorn horns. Katya was the kind of girl that you immediately knew would make a great mom. She had a touch of hippie in her blood. Like, she'd bake cookies with wheat germ and carob chips for a potluck dinner party. Or she'd stew barley soup *and* bake her own whole-grain bread on a snowy Tuesday and get a kick out of sharing the meal with her next-door neighbors.

I was there the night they met. Oliver and I were at a show at Brownie's, a music venue in the East Village that has since shuttered its doors, and Katya asked if she could interview him for her zine. She was a fan of his band, Tuesday Trail. I watched the sparks fly between them and was pleased when he told me that they were dating. Shortly thereafter, they moved to a house in Greenpoint, a total Brooklyn fairy tale.

And now, they were getting married. The plan was for me to grab the Chinatown bus from Philly and roll into Brooklyn on Friday afternoon, meet up with Ricky, and well, that was all I knew. The wedding was the next day, a sunny Saturday in September, in McGolrick Park, a majestic park plopped in the middle of Greenpoint. I'd just started my master's degree in journalism at Temple University, so I was preoccupied with diving back into the rigors of school. However, I was excited to return to my old stomping grounds. It'd been a few years since I moved away from Brooklyn where I lived for two years after college, and I missed the way the sidewalks felt under my feet. More than that, I really missed having access to decent bagels.

Ricky had already flown in a day before from Portland, Oregon, where he'd settled after college. I was genuinely looking forward to seeing the old gang come together as semi-adults. Oliver organized a softball game for all the out-of-towners in McCarren Park, right off the L train in Williamsburg. Unfortunately, I missed the whole thing because of a fire on the subway line. (Ah, New York, you haven't changed one bit. I see you still inconvenience me with the kinds of problems that I'd imagine the society of Mad Max to have! How grand.) I showed up just as everyone was high-fiving and congratulating each other on playing a good game.

I spotted Ricky across the field and he trotted over, giving me the hugest hug.

"Ricky! Hey, buddy!" I smiled as I looked him up and down. He hadn't changed one bit since I'd last seen him. It was like no time had gone by. I'm pretty sure the last time I'd seen him he wore the same thin Pavement T-shirt and dark Levi's. It was classic Ricky.

"Anna Banana! So glad you could make it. But you missed the whole thing." He had dust and dirt on his shirt and pants. Ten bucks says that he slid into a base at some point during the game to crack his team up, because he would totally do something like that for a laugh.

"Yeah, the subway was being a little bitch. But I'm finally here. What's everyone doing now?" I looked around the field to see if there was anyone else I recognized.

"I think we're gonna retreat for a few hours until we meet up later for drinks." Apparently, Ricky was the social director of this event. He should've had a clipboard and a whistle. "Where are you staying?"

Oh shit. I knew I'd forgotten something.

"Actually, funny story: I have no place to stay." As the words left my mouth, I realized that I sounded like a moron.

"Really?" Ricky seemed amused. "So, you clearly put a lot of forethought into this weekend."

"Well, I always stay with Oliver when I come to New York, so I didn't even think about making other plans. And, with starting school a few weeks ago, what can I say? It honestly slipped my mind. In other news, I'm an idiot. Do you know anywhere I could stay?"

"Let me think. Steve might have some room at his place. You know him, right?" He whipped out his cell phone and started dialing Steve's number.

"I don't think I know him, but, yeah, if you could hook that up, that'd be great."

Ricky explained my situation to him. After nodding a lot and exclaiming, "Great!" three times, he snapped his cell phone shut. "He said you could totally stay with him. It's perfect because he lives two blocks from the park where the ceremony is tomorrow. Steve is a cool guy. You'll like him. He used to play with Oliver in Right Way Wrong Turn."

"Cool. Ricky, you're the best." I gave him another hug. After he explained how to get to Steve's house, we parted ways and said we'd catch up in a little bit.

Steve met me outside his house. He was sitting on his stoop strumming an acoustic guitar. If he was trying to avoid the common Brooklyn hipster stereotype of being a shaggy, affected music-loving nerd, he was doing a terrible job at it. Even sitting down, you could tell that he was tall and skinny. I swear to God, there must be a tree in Brooklyn where these kinds of guys are grown. Either that or they fed one of them after midnight and they multiplied like gremlins and took over the first five L train stops.

He was wearing the standard indie-issued thrift-store green T-shirt and raggedy brown cords. It wouldn't surprise me if you told me that he spent his free time riding around in a van with his buddies solving crimes with the help of his dog, Scooby Doo. He was a total ringer for Shaggy, complete with scraggly chin hairs. Good thing he had a mop of red hair so I could at least have a chance of picking him out of a police lineup if it came to that.

"Are you Anna?" He smiled at me.

"I sure am. Are you Steve?" I extended my hand, but he stood up and gave me a hug instead.

"Yup! Any friend of Oliver's is a friend of mine. Welcome to our humble abode. Come on in." I followed him into the building. "Watch your step," he warned as he pulled aside a clear, thick plastic tarp that hung from the ceiling. "The landlord is doing some construction in the foyer, so I apologize for the mess."

"No problem. I'm just so happy that you were able to give me a place to crash. I really appreciate it." I gingerly stepped over the dirty planks of wood and shards of concrete as I followed him into his apartment.

For Greenpoint standards, the place was awesome. I could already picture the Craigslist description:

> Spacious, sunny Greenpoint house available for rent. Ideal place for adorable indie guys with huge record collections. The newly rehabbed kitchen is perfect for making hummus and/or veggie burgers from scratch. The brand-new, brushed-steel refrigerator is well suited to store cheap beers and several varieties of hot sauce. Additionally, there's plenty of room to store dusty musical instruments salvaged from a hometown thrift store and lots of natural sunlight to read Kerouac and pretend that you like it.

I looked around the place, nodding my head in approval. "Wow! You guys have a great place!"

"Aw, thanks. Yeah, we've been really happy here. We totally lucked out with this spot. A quick tour: My room is down those steps in the basement. You can put your stuff there for now. And"—he pointed toward a closed door twenty feet away—"Davy's room is on the other side of the living room."

"Davy?" I asked.

"Yeah, Davy Baxter. Short kid. He used to play with Oliver in a few bands, too, back in the day." Steve put his hand level with his chest as if to approximate Davy's height.

I nodded. Oh, I knew Davy Baxter. He was my old college crush!

"So, it'll just be me, you, and Davy?" I asked.

"Nope. We have one more guy staying with us. His name is Jackson. I think you might know him, too. He dropped his stuff off earlier. I think he's out with Oliver right now."

Yes. I knew Jackson well because he was only my *archenemy.* Now I see that was being hyperbolic, but we had a huge falling-out years ago that was never resolved. Steve did not get the memo that we were archenemies, which I took as yet another sign of our maturity. It was nice to know that my social skirmishes were no longer newsworthy. I was proud of everyone for keeping him in the dark about it; it only helped me look saner.

In yet another testament to how much forethought I put into this weekend, I completely forgot that Jackson would be coming to the wedding. It certainly never occurred to me that we'd be staying in the same place. Shit. I tried to keep my voice from giving away my anxiety. "Oh, cool. Yeah, I know Jackson. Cool, cool." I repeated it, like it suddenly would be cool if I just said it out loud enough times.

A little backstory: Jackson was a cocky, arrogant Southern dude who resembled a beefier version of Owen Wilson. He was a hit with the ladies because he's a natural charmer, but I wasn't interested in him. We seemed to have a mutual unattraction in college: He didn't care for huge brunettes in cargo pants, and conversely, I didn't care for smug Southerners. So it was a draw. We were both friends with Oliver, and that seemed like the only thing we had in common.

Our pleasant acquaintanceship changed the summer before my senior year of college because he didn't return a record player I'd lent him. Sure, it seems innocuous now, but it wasn't my record player; I was watching it for someone else, which put me in a pickle. When I lent it to him, I explained that it wasn't mine and that if he did borrow it, he'd have to return it within the week. He swore up and down that he'd return it right away. But he didn't. He dodged my phone calls for almost two months until he finally returned it. The whole ordeal culminated with my calling him an asshole. Things had been chilly between us ever since.

Since I was dramatic, I told everyone with a pair of ears what a dickhead he was. "I did him a favor and he abused my trust!" I'd say, my friends nodding along, commiserating. I declared him my archenemy and avoided him like the plague. Unfortunately, it made dorm room parties awkward. I tried to coerce my friends to pick sides, but no one did. They just shrugged and pretended nothing had happened because it wasn't their battle to fight. I see that now. Besides, if I had pressed the issue, it would have just made me look like a psycho, so I buried my hatred for him so deep that he became my secret archenemy. It was so secret, I'm not even sure if Jackson knew about it.

Last I heard, he'd run for mayor of a small town outside Nashville and lost. Even that story annoyed me because he was the type of guy to run for political office just so he'd have a quirky story to tell a beautiful woman at a cocktail party. He was also the type of guy who'd buy a girl's friends drinks to win them over so she'd let her guard down and agree to date him. He was too calculating. The mere mention of his name made my skin crawl.

Steve told me that there was going to be a prewedding drinkfest at the Levee on Third and Bedford Avenue, which was in the heart of Williamsburg. I tossed on a swingy yellow dress and little black flats. After enjoying a quick beer at his place, Steve and I walked over to join the rest of the gang.

The Levee was a small, loud bar with a killer jukebox. As we walked in, "Born to Run" echoed off the sticky walls, a working-class anthem reverberating in a leisure town. This was the kind of bar where bad decisions could be made effortlessly. Every town has a bar like that, with great tunes and cheap beers. But every bar in this neighborhood felt like it was made to cater to bad ideas. I used to live in Williamsburg, so I speak from experience here. Brimming with artists and young professionals and generally beautiful people, these streets were best traversed by the young and carefree. Williamsburg is all about confidence, and I was confident that I was going to have fun that night.

I caught sight of my friends in the back. They had taken over a few tables and were engaged in several half-hugs and belly laughs.

I sat down next to Ricky and looked around the room. Oliver was at the bar surrounded by his high school buddies, pounding back shots. Steve hovered over the jukebox, hunting for a song to play. Then, it happened. I locked eyes with Jackson, my archenemy. I narrowed mine. And, to my shock, he widened his. His eyebrows practically flew off his forehead, they were arched up so high. He immediately came over and gave me a hug, totally thrilled to see me. I was in too much shock to resist. My former archenemy had extended an olive branch. If he remembered that he was my archenemy, he certainly didn't show it.

"Well, I'll be! Anna Goldfarb as I live and breathe! It is so good to see you, darlin'." He hugged me so tight it felt like he was genuinely surprised that I was still alive. As he hugged me, I stopped in my tracks and started wildly sniffing the air like a bloodhound, trying to trace the scent. *Damn*, son! *Someone* had invested in some fancy cologne.

I'm not sure if it was a present from his mom last Christmas or from an ex with excellent taste or if he'd strutted his little butt down to Nordstrom and picked it out himself, but I just wanna say that smelling him was an absolute pleasure.

I wish I could capture smells somehow because I would've uploaded it to my phone, e-mailed it to myself, printed it out, and framed it on the motherfucking wall. I want to live in a world where *all* men's necks smell like his. Can we make that happen, please? Can't Bono make a few phone calls and get that ball rolling? Fuck, I'd have paid a month's rent just to roll around in Jackson's dirty T-shirts. He smelled like a hip-hop mogul. He smelled the *exact opposite* of how I'd imagine Matthew McConaughey to smell like. *Shiiiiiiit.*

If this were a transaction on eBay, I'd say, "A++++. Would smell again!" And I'd mean every word. Bravo, sir. *Bravo.*

"Hey, Jackson! Yeah, it's been a while," I agreed.

"It's been more than a while. Damn, girl! Hold on. Whatcha drinkin'? Let me get you something."

"Oh, wow. A beer would be great. Whatever you're having, I'll have." He zipped over to the bar and quickly returned with both a beer and two double shots of Jameson whiskey, one for him and one for me.

"Wow! Thanks, Jackson." I followed him to a corner table.

He raised his shot glass. "To old friends!"

"To old friends!" I repeated, lifting my shot glass up. Was this guy for real? We gulped it down and quickly winced as it slid down our gullets.

"So, tell me. What the hell have you been up to?" He leaned in close to me as he waited for my answer.

"Well, after school, I moved to Philly. Right now, I'm into drinking and causing trouble." He laughed at that.

"That's so funny. In college you were always so serious."

"Yeah, I was pretty uptight."

"Are you still writing?" He remembered that I used to be a freelance writer back in college. Sweet.

"Actually, I just started journalism school at Temple a few weeks ago. So far I really like it. But enough about me. What the hell is up with you? Where have you been? I heard you ran for mayor. Whaaaaaat? That's insane."

He took a slug of his beer. "Yup, I sure did. I would've been the youngest mayor in the town's history if I'd won, too."

"Oh, wow. Was it a close race?"

"Ha! Not at all. I got pummeled in the polls," he laughed.

"But, it was cool. I've also done some writing. I freelanced for *Esquire* for a while there. But, now I'm working for the AP as their Bolivia correspondent. I've been stationed there for, damn, almost a year now."

"That's . . . amazing," I stuttered. "Seriously, that's amazing." I was doing a terrible job of being unimpressed.

"It's all right. It pays the bills." He took another pull from his beer bottle. "I'll tell you what was cool. I got to meet Hugo Chávez for a story I worked on."

"No way!" My eyes were wide. "How'd that happen? That's crazy!"

"Yeah, I had to bribe a few local officials to get access to him. He's shorter than you'd think." I'd never thought of Hugo Chávez's height before, but I nodded along like I had.

A waitress came by, and Jackson ordered us another round and began spinning tales of his work in Bolivia. Despite myself I was enthralled, hanging on every word. I'm not sure how much time had passed, but there was an army of empty beer bottles in front of us and the crowd at the bar had thinned out a bit. Oliver had left earlier, probably in preparation for his big day tomorrow. Damn! I didn't even get to say hello. I guess I was so engaged by Jackson's stories that I had tuned everything else out. But I did notice that every time we finished a round of drinks, Jackson would inch his chair closer to mine.

He reached into a bag on the floor, pulled out an expensive bottle of fifteen-year-old whiskey, and rested it on the table in front of us. "I brought this for Oliver tonight, but he's gone now and there's nothing wrong with us having a little taste, is there?"

"Nope. Nothing wrong with that," I agreed.

He looked both ways to make sure no bartenders were looking, and then he filled our shot glasses almost to the top. I figured that this would be a good time to clear the air.

"You know, I hated you in college," I blurted out.

I watched his face as he took back the shot. He slammed the empty shot glass on the table. "You called me an asshole." He definitely remembered.

"You *were* an asshole!" I protested.

"I was an asshole," he agreed. "I'm sorry, darlin'. You're right. I was a total asshole. What can I say? It wasn't your record player and I should have respected that. I was a royal dickhead. Now, how can I make it up to you?" He leaned in even closer to me.

"This whiskey is a good start," I said as I slid my empty glass toward him. He laughed and poured us both another shot.

His Southern drawl, which used to grate, now put me at ease. My eyes twinkled every time he called me "darlin'."

"You know, it's a shame that we didn't get a chance to reconcile sooner," he mused. "Think of all the fun we could've had."

I didn't say anything; I just let that soak into my brain. What was going on? Was I attracted to him? Maybe. I wasn't expecting this to happen.

Before I figured out how I felt about it, he stood up, grabbed the half-empty whiskey bottle, and said, "Let's get out of here."

I didn't resist when he took my hand as we walked out.

"Wait here, I'll grab Steve," I said, walking back into the bar to round him up. It didn't take long to find him; he was arguing with a friend about Radiohead's latest record review on Pitchfork, an influential music site. In case I wasn't sure I was in Brooklyn before, hearing two educated adults bicker over a record review pretty much laid it out. Thankfully, Steve was ready to take off, too.

After saying our good-byes, we all walked back to Steve's house giggling like young drunks. Steve retreated into his room downstairs, but Jackson and I made our way to the living room couch. Spoiler alert: We couldn't keep our hands off each other. We stayed up all night, talking and kissing and talking and kissing until the sun came up, when we finally passed out.

The morning light streamed in, illuminating the living room. We rubbed our eyes and got ready for Oliver's wedding. Jackson headed over first; I stayed behind with Steve and finished dolling up. I tossed on a black wraparound dress and pearls and then scurried over to McGolrick Park just in time for the ceremony.

As I took my seat, I caught sight of Jackson. He had red, tired eyes and was wearing a black tux. He was stationed at the front, by the altar. My God, I had just (inadvertently) hooked up with the best man! Did I win a prize? It felt like I'd hit the five-hundred-point hole in Skee-Ball. I won the Best Man Bingo!

The wedding was lovely. I sat next to Ricky and cried a little bit when Oliver and Katya pledged eternal love to each other. Ricky gave me a crinkly tissue from his pocket and assured me that my mascara didn't smear after I dabbed at my tears.

The reception was down the street in a Polish reception hall. It felt like the entire building was made out of frosting; huge, frilly white moldings decorated the walls. Oliver and Katya had hired an authentic soul band to provide musical entertainment, and entertain they did. There were four guys in blindingly white zoot suits with full-on Jheri curls strutting around like they were on *Soul Train*. They had harmonies and choreography to spare. They also had a female singer who looked like Sheila E. with teased hair and white eye shadow, which expertly matched her white pantsuit.

The band sang the hell out of a catalog of soul classics. Oliver even joined them onstage and pulled a Phil Collins: He played drums and sang on a cover of the song "Build Me Up, Buttercup." I stood by the side of the stage with Ricky and cheered him on.

For dinner, I was seated at a table with all of my old college friends. My buddy Wyatt was there; I hadn't seen him since graduation. He was the one who wrote me the breakup letter so many years ago. He talked a mile a minute and cracked me up. I told him that if he were a podcast, I'd download him every week.

Jackson was seated up front along with the bride and groom. We made eye contact a few times and smiled at each other. For the most part, I bopped around, shoveling food onto my plate, dancing and drinking.

I was pleased when Wyatt asked me to dance. Of course I said yes. A total goofball, he spun me around the dance floor like I was a rag doll. The fact that I'd probably had a bottle of wine by then made me especially ready to boogie. Everything was going great until he tried to execute a dip, aka the worst dance move ever. The laws of physics conspired against us: His 5'7" soft frame was no match for my 6'1". He placed his hand on my lower back and tried to bend me backward. Immediately, it was evident that he'd misjudged a few key things: namely my flexibility and his strength.

He held me in the dip position for about one second until I felt his biceps start to quiver. Then, in the middle of the dance floor, with everyone watching us, he dropped me. It felt like it happened in slow motion, like an elephant going down after being hit by a tranquilizer gun. I went down. Hard.

As I was falling, I made eye contact with Katya's grandmother. Her mouth was wide open and she looked horrified, like I'd just grabbed the pope's butt during Christmas mass.

Unfortunately, Oliver's new in-laws had front-row seats to my wipeout. I landed with a thud, totally spread-eagled in front of the entire table, which got an eyeful of my black cotton Jockey for Hers flashing around like a surrender flag.

Wyatt tried to help me get up from the floor, but he was too weak to pull me up. He almost did it, but then he lost his grip and I fell back on the ground again. After a few failed rescue attempts, I finally rolled over onto my knees and slowly got up like the lady that I am. With Wyatt wiping away tears on the back of his sleeve from laughing so hard, I apologized to the entire table.

I looked around the room, and it was clear that the party was winding down. I grabbed my purse and left to find Steve to go back to his house. I didn't find him, but I found Davy Baxter. At 5'5", he looked just as he had in college, so many years ago.

He looked handsome, like a less-greasy, shorter version of Ethan Hawke in *Reality Bites*. My face lit up.

"Hey, Davy, have you seen Steve? I'm not sure if you heard, but I'm staying at your place tonight."

"Hey, Anna. Yeah, I have no idea where Steve went. I was just gonna head back, too. Wanna go with me?"

"Sure, that'd be great."

Once we got back to his place, we plopped on the living room couch. Davy took out his laptop and went to check his MySpace page. (This was in 2006, before Facebook made MySpace a deserted Internet playground except for mallpunk bands and divorced dads in flyover states.)

I looked over his shoulder at his page and remarked that he should customize his top eight. He didn't know how to do it, so I showed him how, even bumping it up to a top sixteen. To thank me for my tech support, he placed me in the thirteenth position of his top sixteen. It was a bit of a scrolldown, but I was pleased with the gesture.

Shit. Here I was, kicking it with my college crush, nestled in his top sixteen to boot. Life was good. Steve and Jackson came home a little bit later, so after everyone got their nap on, we got ready for the afterparty, at a bar on Seventh and Driggs. I changed into a short red dress. The guys tossed on some jeans. We rolled in to celebrate with the newlyweds.

After a little bit, I found Davy sitting in a booth, fiddling with a digital camera. I slid next to him.

"Take a picture of me," I demanded. He complied, shifted a

little to the side to get a better angle, and snapped a picture. The flash was bright.

"Now take another one of both of us." Without saying a word, he scooted next to me, extended his arm, leaned into the frame, and took a picture of us together. He put the camera down but still stayed close to me. He was so close, I could smell his cologne, which was still on him from the wedding that afternoon. I liked it.

"Wanna get outta here?" he asked.

"God, yes."

Davy took my hand and I followed him to the door, turning around to catch a glimpse of Jackson at the bar, craning his neck to see where I was going.

*Are you leaving?* he mouthed.

I nodded.

*With him?* he mouthed back.

I nodded again. Then I shrugged. Sorry, former archenemy! I had the chance to make out with someone on my kiss wish list who didn't live in Bolivia. Besides, Davy was so cute, and holding hands with him felt awesome, like finding a winning lotto ticket that I thought I'd lost.

I thought we would head back to his house, but he took a sharp turn down a desolate block. "Where are we going?"

"My favorite place. You'll love it."

This "favorite place" that Davy took me to was a hockey bar called the Penalty Box. It was situated beneath an underpass, but it might as well have been located in Mordor. If I had to describe this place, I'd go with "smoky coke den." Underneath the copious amounts of neon beer signage, we were surrounded by the kinds of people who looked like they didn't wear sunscreen or make flossing their teeth a priority. It felt like we were at a Jerry Springer taping. I think we were the only people in the place who didn't owe child support. It was safe to say that I didn't quite fit in with the deadbeat-dad aesthetic the Penalty Box so expertly cultivated.

Davy picked out two bar stools by the TV. A hockey game was on and it was loud, competing with the lively conversation around us. We ordered the cheapest beers in the place.

"Do you think she's on MySpace?' Davy pondered.

"Who?"

"The singer of the band. She was really hot."

"Which band?" I was confused.

"The band at Oliver's wedding. The singer lady. She was so talented. I went up to talk to her. She told me that she's thirty-five. Is that too old for me?"

"Are you kidding? Is this a joke?" Davy was on another planet.

"No, she was really hot. Do you think she'd go out with me?"

"Um, do you wanna go back and ask her?"

"Nah." He didn't pick up on my sarcasm. "Besides, she's probably gone anyway." He'd honestly considered leaving me at the Penalty Box and going back to the Polish venue to ask her out. I was floored.

"So, you take me to this stink hole and you're talking my ear off about another girl? Are you serious?" I was downright offended. If he hadn't been so good-looking, I would've stomped right out. This felt just like college; I still couldn't keep his attention. Challenge accepted, Davy.

I grabbed Davy's hand and shushed him.

"We have one night together. Let's make the most of it." I tried to sound sultry, but I think I just sounded demented.

"Yeah, but do you think she's on—"

"I said be quiet. Stop talking about this girl." I wished I could've given Davy a personality transplant, or at least a muzzle. He was so much better with his mouth shut. This was the thanks I got for formatting his top sixteen?

Well, we got hammered at the hockey bar. I didn't listen to a word he said; I just tried to pretend that I was on a better date, sipping better beers with a better guy. After a while, we decided to go back to his place. It was a ten-minute walk but it took a bit longer because he'd take three steps forward and one step back. His little frame couldn't handle the day of drinking.

We finally got to his house, and it took him another five minutes to find his keys. As he put his key in the door, he turned around from the top step and kissed me. To his credit, it was a perfect kiss. I felt like I'd fallen into a pile of pillows. I was also tired and drunk, so anything probably would've felt good at that point.

Once inside, we went straight to his room. He expertly navigated the mess on the floor, but I stumbled on something right away. I flicked on his overhead light and to my horror, it looked like a garage sale had puked all over the place. There was junk everywhere. His clothing was half-strewn in the dresser, like zombie shirts poking out of their drawer graves. Dirty dishes teetered precariously on his desk. I gasped. I've seen tidier crack houses. Being in his room was like being stuck in Charles Manson's brain.

He was already halfway across the room. "Come to bed," he urged. I tiptoed through the muck to his bed. Unfortunately, there weren't any sheets on his mattress. I'm pretty sure even prisoners have sheets. I felt like I was lying down in a greasy pizza box.

I curled up next to him and we kissed for exactly four minutes before he passed out. Turning over on my side, I slipped my arm around his waist. I was the outer spoon, bringing him into my chest like a stuffed animal. That was when I noticed that his pillows were flat. I tried to fold one over itself to give my head more support, but it was no use. I felt like I was resting on Olive Oyl's bony knee. There was no way I was going to be able to sleep in this clutter.

I reached over to tug at his comforter and get a bit of warmth when I felt that all-too-familiar scratchy, thin, cheap fabric: It's from IKEA, isn't it? *It is*. I knew it. I fucking called it. To paraphrase the Aaron Neville and Linda Ronstadt power ballad, I don't know much, but I *know* this shitty comforter.

For the record, my comforter on my bed is fluffy and light, like Dr. Emmett Brown's hair. It's a neutral color because, unlike Davy, I don't need orange rectangles and burnt sienna ovals on my bedding. I get that he's artsy; his bed doesn't have to rub it in my face.

It was dotted with cigarette burns from almost a decade of

late-night gabfests with a parade of ex-girlfriends. It felt like I was brushing up against a hobo's crusty nostril every time the fabric scratched my skin.

Not to be too dramatic, but the one-two punch of a shitty IKEA bedspread and flat pillows is my own personal version of Guantanamo Bay. I frowned at the lackluster bedding, sighing heavily as I made the best of it.

Then, I heard Steve's and Jackson's voices through the walls chattering away in the next room. They must have just gotten home from the party. I started to feel bad for blowing Jackson off but not bad enough to go out there and say hi or anything. That was when it hit me that I'd hooked up with two-thirds of this household within twenty-four hours. I was like a bad math problem.

There was definitely no chance of sleeping a wink because the thought of seeing both Davy *and* Jackson over breakfast bagels was a little too awkward for me to endure. I lay awake all night, unable to catch one wink of shut-eye. Sleeping with Davy wasn't nearly as much fun as I'd hoped, but I was proud of myself for finally being able to cross him off my kiss wish list. I comforted myself with the thought that it was better than most wedding souvenirs. Go, me!

Around six A.M., I quietly gathered my things and left a note on the kitchen table thanking my hosts for their generous hospitality. I even drew a red heart on it using my lipstick because I'm classy.

I slipped out of the house like a cat burglar and power-walked to the subway like I was leaving the scene of a crime.

Thirty-five minutes later, I was standing on a dingy corner in Chinatown, chewing on a toasted everything bagel smeared with cream cheese, waiting to catch the first bus back to Philly.

If this were an episode of *Full House*, Danny Tanner would sit on the edge of my bed as we went over what I learned from this event. Soft music would play and I'd tell him that I learned that I'm not the kind of girl to turn down a willing fella on her kiss wish list, even if he's infatuated with a woman who wears white eye shadow and even if it makes it awkward for every other person in his house. So, I guess you could say that I knew myself eighty-six percent of the way by the end of the weekend. Figuring out the rest was Future Anna's problem.

# CHAPTER 8

# The High Cost of a Free Sandwich

Recently, I've developed a few disturbing habits. First, I've been dabbling in petty theft. Don't worry, I'm not pulling a Winona Ryder, stuffing my handbag full of pricey garments at Bloomingdale's. As far as my thievery goes, I steal pretty stupid shit. Mostly, I've been stealing a bottle or two of beer from a house party or backstage area. It's a little trophy for the road. Dexter has microscopic glass slides of his victims' blood; I have a lukewarm Corona in my purse.

I tell myself that it's not that bad in the scheme of things. I don't even know if swiping a beer is an actual legal offense. I doubt anyone would press charges over one measly beer bottle. In the spectrum of bad houseguest behavior, stealing a beer from someone's fridge ranks somewhere between accidentally breaking a wineglass and puking in the host's hamper. So why do it? Why take the risk? Because it's a frosty present for my future self. I think ahead to a time when I come home from a long day at work and see a stolen Sierra Nevada chillin' in my fridge. That stolen beer is an investment in my future happiness. A brewed 401(k), if you will.

My second disturbing habit is that I've been craving sandwiches late at night. I'm like a portly sitcom dad: I pretty much need a sandwich in my face at that exact minute the bars close down for Philly's two A.M. curfew. Starting at midnight, it's all I think about. *Where am I gonna get this sandwich? What kind will I get? Do I want honey roasted turkey or plain? Should I buy another beer or save my money and spring for a footlong?* I'm weighing the pros and cons of partying longer with stuffing my face in an hour. I'm like a thoughtful gremlin; it's insane.

I'm not proud of either of these things. And it hasn't escaped my attention that if I combined the two, I'd basically be Jean Valjean from *Les Misérables*. But, thankfully, my life isn't a Broadway musical about the French Revolution, so I'm in the clear. For now.

One night, I was at an afterparty for a large tech conference in downtown Philly. It was like Mardi Gras for the Twitterati; people were updating their statuses to make everyone aware that they were having a blast. (Because if nerds know anything, it's that it's not a good time until it's documented, tweeted, and ignored.)

The organizers had invited me to deejay the event, which I was happy to do. It was my first time behind the turntables, but I didn't let that intimidate me. I decided to have a nineties theme to my set because I never get to hear that kind of music when I go out. So with *Reality Bites* streaming on a screen behind me, I regaled the bar with a lively mix of the Cardigans, Nirvana, and R.E.M. Thankfully, the venue paired me up with an experienced deejay who tweaked the levels and fiddled with the necessary knobs so I didn't make a total fool of myself in front of the packed crowd.

After my set, I made my way to the bar to slam a beer, celebrating a job well done and trying to figure out if I should head over to the Wawa for a six-inch turkey on wheat with cheese, pickles, lettuce, and tomato, or go the extra mile down to South Philly and hit up Jim's for one of their fabulous cheesesteaks. I was by the bar trying to flag the bartender down when my friend Rosie suddenly appeared next to me. She was very drunk.

Swinging her arm around my shoulder, she slurred. "Annnnnnna. This guy right here in the black leather jacket behind me? His name is Sam. I can't believe I'm telling you this, but he's so rich. Like, *so rich*! And he likes you. He was just telllllllling me about how he thinks you're cute." She turned her head to let out a burp. "'Scuse me."

I nodded. Clearly, a situation was developing here, and I'm not talking about the one in her stomach. At that moment, I took a second to high-five myself in my head because I had chosen to wear my polka-dot dress to the party. A total boner-grower, the sweetheart neckline showed off my rack perfectly. I smiled wide as Rosie continued, although she didn't have to; I was already sold on the idea of meeting him.

"You should talk to him. He just moved here from D.C. and he thinks you're prrrrrretty. He's staying at the Four Seasons Hotel. You need to meet him. This could be your future husband or something. He's Jewish like you. Oh my God, you guys are gonna have the cutest babies."

I closed my eyes for a second and imagined my babies with this mystery man whose face I had never seen. Yes, they were cute in my head!

"He's sitting at the end of the bar." Rosie smelled like a bar mat.

"Oh, wow. Thanks for the heads-up." A rich dude? Here? What luck! Rosie is *hooking me up*! I turned to peep this fine specimen, my potential Daddy Warbucks in leather.

My smile evaporated quickly. At the end of the bar teetering on a stool was a man who looked like Jerry Seinfeld with adult acne and huge, greasy Jeffrey Dahmer eyeglasses. He resembled a melted Elvis Costello. And, to my horror, he was wearing a *baggy* leather jacket, the kind old people buy at Costco. He looked like he was in a dad band. It was not hot.

I felt betrayed by this leather jacket description, swindled even. How can something made of leather be so wimpy? There was nothing tough about this guy or his jacket. I wanted to strip it off him, stuff it in a garbage can, and set it on fire. Honestly, I would've preferred if he had just shown up in a barrel and suspenders. Hell, even a unitard would've been an improvement. That would've been a better look for him than that baggy leather jacket.

As I got closer, I saw that he had stiff, spiky bangs. I immediately pictured him in front of his mirror applying product to the front of his head, sculpting his bangs to get them all crispy and pointy like that. It was goofy! Honestly, he looked like a boy band's understudy. I'll admit that I thought that this look was cool for, like, five minutes in early 2000. (If you must know, it was during the video for 'N Sync's "Bye Bye Bye.") But that was eons ago! I don't understand why guys continue to do this to themselves.

Stiff, spiky bangs are *the worst.* I would rather die than have them touch any part of my face or body. The only time this look is acceptable is if you are a six-year-old named Calvin with a stuffed tiger as a best friend. Only then will those spiky bangs get a pass.

However, fashion faux pas aside, this guy was rich. Rosie said so. And then the lightbulb went off above my head: I'm going to make this rich guy buy me a fancy sandwich. Screw this turkey sub shit. Maybe this sandwich will have caviar on it, maybe a shaved truffle or two. Maybe it will have something exotic that I don't even know about yet! Operation Fancy Sandwich was a go. I walked toward him with visions of delicious snacks dancing in my head.

"Hi! I'm Anna. Nice to meet you." I stuck out my hand and he reflexively stuck his out, too. I hated his handshake. It was just a mess from the limp start to the awkward, clammy finish. It was like I was meeting Bernie from *Weekend at Bernie's.* I actually looked behind him to see if Andrew McCarthy was propping him up.

Not only was his hand inert and moist like a dead cod, but it felt feminine. And slender. And small. And pampered. He basically had a Barbie hand. The heaviest thing he had probably lifted was cream puffs out of a pink pastry box, or maybe a teacup at a little girl's tea party. I couldn't imagine that those hands had ever chopped wood or sealed a bank merger deal. I shuddered just thinking about those hands touching any part of my body. Those were the unsexiest hands I've ever felt. He had the hands of an Olsen twin.

But there were possible fancy sandwiches on the horizon, so I had to soldier on. He stood up to talk to me and he almost fell over. He was totally trashed, just super drunk. "Hi, Annnnnna." Oh great, another slurrer. He was shorter than me by several inches and his black shoes had a thick rubber sole in an effort to toss another inch to his petite frame. I didn't expect him to know this about me, but I can't stand when short guys wear lifts. He might as well wear a neon shirt that says *I'm insecure about my height.* I like my short guys out and proud. This would have to be one more detail I'd have to overlook if we were going to be seen in public together. That list was getting longer by the minute.

As I was calculating how many things about his appearance I was unhappy with, he looked at me like I was a piece of IKEA furniture that didn't come with assembly instructions. I was going to have to take charge if this sandwich was going to happen.

"Let's get out of here and grab a bite to eat. There's a great place around the corner," I semi-shouted into his ear over the loud music blaring from the speakers.

He stared at me for a second, like he forgot where he was and why I was talking to him. I smiled. He blinked. Then he said, "Sure."

I followed him out of the bar, which had about twenty large concrete steps down to the street. Those stairs are notoriously perilous for anyone who wears stilettos or is prone to spells of vertigo. As soon as Sam's foot touched the first step, he flopped down the stairs in a wipeout so epic it would've made Humpty Dumpty cringe. As he smacked onto the sidewalk, his glasses tumbled into the middle of the road. I gasped.

"Holy shit! Are you okay?" I raced down the steps and picked him up by the elbows. Once he was steady on his feet, I bolted into the street to retrieve his glasses. He was clearly rattled by the spill but said he was fine. I was surprised his frail frame didn't shatter on impact or that his limbs didn't snap off his body like dry kindling.

It was clear that I couldn't leave him in this drunken stupor. He was so hammered that he'd probably walk into oncoming traffic, and I didn't want that on my conscience. His stupid jacket and thick shoe soles had already shown me that he was prone to making terrible decisions, so I didn't put walking into traffic past him. To paraphrase the ugly girl in *The Goonies*, I felt like I was babysitting without getting paid.

"Seriously, let's grab a bite. I know a great place around the corner." I pointed to the end of the street and pulled his arm gently to follow me. It was getting late; soon restaurants would be closing. I had to hurry this up.

"I'm staying at the Four Seasons. Let's just go there. *Taxi!*" He flagged a taxi down and before I could protest, we spilled into a cab that had pulled up beside us. "Four Seasons, please," he instructed the cabdriver.

After a few silent minutes, I asked, "So, what do you do?"

"I invented a computer chip a few years ago. It's a pretty big deal." His thick glasses reflected the glow of the streetlights we zoomed past. It seemed that I had snagged my own Bill Gates! Well, if Bill Gates were 5'7", was dressed like a hall monitor, and was blindingly drunk at one A.M. on a Thursday.

"Oh really? How much of a big deal?" This guy could barely stand ten minutes ago and now he's boasting? I think I liked him better when he was just the quiet drunken guy who fell down a lot.

"You ever hear of CalmStreaming.com?"

"No." I shrugged.

"Well, I founded that site. We netted a few million last year." He could hardly keep his head up and the words came really slowly and kinda muddled. It felt like I was listening to a hacked version of Teddy Ruxpin that was on its last dying battery and only played a prerecorded message about his net worth. With that, he slumped over and hit his head on the headrest. The impact jolted him awake.

"So, why are you here in Philly? This isn't exactly Silicon Valley."

"My company set up offices here, so I'm overseeing the transition. I've been at the Four Seasons for a week now. In my opinion, it's the best hotel in this city. Did you know that they have a swimming pool? And a Jacuzzi? I'm getting a really great rate, too. And the staff is so friendly. They even leave little mints on my—*hiccup*—pillow."

"That's, like, every hotel. That's just what hotels do. I hate to burst your bubble, Sam, but the mint thing is pretty common."

"No, but the Four Seasons is the best of the best. I always stay here when I come to Philly. And their mints are imported from, fuck, I don't remember. But they're delicious. I wouldn't expect you to understand." He sounded like a snobby ad for the hotel.

"Did you go to school in D.C.?" I asked, racking my brain for something else to talk about. I should've kept quiet. Hell, I should've jumped out of the cab altogether. But, I didn't.

"No, I went to Princeton for my undergraduate degree. Then, I got three graduate degrees at MIT." He didn't even look at me when he spoke, and he certainly didn't ask me any questions about myself. Just as I noticed that he wasn't looking at me, I felt his hand on my leg. This guy had to be kidding.

"I think you're pretty." Now he was looking at me. He moved his hand up my thigh a little bit, which felt like an eel slithering across my leg.

I laughed nervously and batted his hand away. "Oh, wow. Thanks. Look at that: We're here."

The imposing golden doors of the hotel brushed open noiselessly, and I made a beeline straight for the restaurant toward the back of the hotel. I nodded at an attendant as I walked past, trying to appear like the kind of girl who'd stay at a hotel like this. I'm not sure what fancy hotel guests look like, but they probably don't waltz in at one A.M. flanked by drunk nerds. Sam struggled to keep up with my brisk pace.

The restaurant looked like the inside of my grandma's purse; neat, plain, and very mauve. "A table for two, please!" I cheerfully told the maitre d'.

"I'm sorry, but we're closed," he sniffed.

"But those people over there are eating." I pointed toward the back where six guys sat with their ties loosened and snifters in hand. Sam swayed back and forth but thankfully didn't topple over.

"Well, the kitchen closes at one A.M. It's now"—he checked his watch—"one oh three A.M., so I'm sorry. However, you are still able to order room service. That's available around the clock." He gave us a tight smile.

"Okay. Thanks." I debated my options: I could either abandon the mission and secure my own pedestrian sandwich elsewhere, or I could ride it out and see what kind of amazing sandwich I could order from the hotel. I'd already invested this much energy; I couldn't leave now. And seeing that I was curious about my room service options, room service seemed like my best bet at this point. I looked at Sam and said the last six words I had any desire to say to him: "Okay, let's go to your room."

He didn't even hesitate. "Follow me." We shuffled into the

elevator and he scanned the buttons for his floor. "Wait, there's no twelve here. I'm staying on the twelfth floor. What the fuck?" He was right; the buttons stopped at ten. I didn't know what to tell him. We exited the elevator and marched straight up to the reception desk. Well, I marched. Sam stumbled.

"Excuse me," Sam said to the clerk, "but my—*hiccup*—floor isn't here." Oh great. It's hard to take a drunk guy seriously, but a hiccupping drunk guy? He might as well be wearing a dunce cap.

"Which floor are you staying on, sir?" The guy behind the desk seemed concerned. It's probably not every day that a floor up and disappears.

"The twelfth floor."

"May I see your key, please?"

Sam plopped his hotel key on the desk. It made a faint *ting* noise. Then he hiccupped again.

The desk attendant picked up the key card and examined it. "Sir, this is a key to the Ritz-Carlton. You are in the wrong hotel." Sam took the key and stared at it like he'd just found out that the key was his biological father. I guess MIT must not have covered *remembering which hotel you're staying at* in his rigorous coursework.

Sam honestly looked surprised by the news that he wasn't staying at the Four Seasons. He took his key back and thanked the guy at the reception desk. I shook my head. I couldn't believe he'd hyped up this hotel so much and wasn't even staying here. What kind of person forgets the hotel he's been staying at for a week? And how did he magically decide that he was staying at the Four Seasons? He didn't even address the mix-up; he just walked outside and flagged down another taxi.

The Ritz-Carlton was five blocks away. In the cab, he tried to put his hand on my leg again. And I swatted it away. Again.

"You really didn't know the hotel you were staying at?" I asked, quizzically.

He shrugged and hiccupped. I turned to face him. I wasn't going to let this go.

"They don't even sound alike. The Four Seasons and the Ritz-Carlton are two totally different places. I assume you checked in. They gave you a key. Your luggage is there. And what kills me is that you seemed so confident about the whole thing! Your hotel was, like, the only thing you've talked to me about all night." I searched his face for any reaction. He didn't give me any.

This hotel was just as beautiful as the last one. It had the same huge doors, the same silent attendants, and, unfortunately, the same closed restaurant situation. However, unlike the last hotel, this elevator had a twelfth floor.

As soon as we entered his room, he kicked off his huge shoes and immediately turned around and tried to shove his tongue in my mouth. It was a spin move he must've learned from watching a Michael Jackson video or something because it was one fluid motion: the ol' kick and slobber.

I instinctively put my hands up to deflect his advances. "Let's order some food!" I suggested.

He ignored me and said, "Come here." With that, he planted

the greasiest, sloppiest, wettest kiss on my lips. It felt like I had plunged my face into a bowl full of buttered noodles. I pushed him away. "Let's order food now," I insisted.

Sam frowned, then walked over to the phone. He picked up the receiver and pushed three buttons. "Hello. Room service. Thank you." [*hiccup*]

Now that food was in my near future, I became visibly excited. "Is there a menu? Can I get something with seafood?" After all this bullshit, I upgraded my sandwich sights to more extravagant fare. I wanted to eat something with claws, something caught in cold waters.

Sam mumbled into the phone, "I'll have a roast beef sandwich. Yes, with French fries. Uh-huh."

"Get something with crab!" I chirped. "Maybe a lobster?" I was really reaching for the seafood stars here.

"And a side salad. Yes. Room twelve sixteen. Thank you." He hung up the phone.

I was pissed. "Well, what about me? What am I gonna eat?" I felt like I was going to cry. I was so hungry I could've eaten the strap off my purse.

Sam looked at me. "Well, you just cost me two hundred dollars. Hope you're happy." He came over and sat beside me on the edge of the bed.

"How on *earth* could a roast beef sandwich that I didn't even want cost two hundred dollars?" I couldn't believe this guy! I was kind enough to make sure he didn't walk into traffic and/or have his glasses smashed and this was how he thanked me?

He wound his arms around my waist and kissed my neck. I pushed him away.

"Dude," I said, firmly.

"Shhhh. Don't worry about it." He put a finger to my lips as though that would somehow make me forget that I'd just had his slimy lips on my body. He was not a hypnotist; he couldn't just make me magically forget what I'd felt by waving his finger around.

"I think you're pretty. There's, like, ten things that I like about you." He took my face in his hands and tried to kiss me again.

"Ten things? Like what?"

"For one thing, I think you're pretty. And I like your hair." [*hiccup*]

"Okay. That's two. Do you even remember my name?" This is how I can tell how drunk a guy is. It's my own sobriety field test.

"It begins with an *S*, right? Stella? No, wait. Sasha?"

I didn't want to correct him. "Yes, it's Sasha. Sure."

With that, he took his pants off and tossed them on a chair, revealing thin black socks and black boxers. This was the worst striptease I'd ever seen. He pulled back a corner of the bedspread.

"Care to, uh, join me?" I think he was trying to sound seductive, but he just sounded desperate. This come-on was more of a *Come on, there's no way this is going to work*.

"Not really. I'm good," I said and looked around the room nervously.

It didn't matter because he couldn't hear me; he was too busy trying to detangle himself from his white T-shirt. The front was pulled up over his head and his arms were trapped inside it. He looked like he was wrestling a tiny ghost. With his vision obscured, he tripped over one of his chunky shoes and crashed into the bed face-first.

After a few minutes, he finally managed to pull his shirt off. And as he scooted under the covers, I got a look at his saggy, untoned chest. He had tiny nipples the size of nickels and wiry, thick hair all over his back, a total ape cape. What woman could resist this? After he rustled around for a few seconds, his boxer shorts joined the pile on the chair.

Save for his black socks, he was naked. I tried to suppress my gag reflex. The fact that I was still interested in eating after seeing his hairy, pale thighs is a testament to the severity of my hunger.

"You know what we need? Music! I'll put some on." I bounded across the room and fiddled with the radio, scanning the dial for the least sexy music I could find. Where's a twenty-four-hour polka station when you need it? While I was scanning the dial, my least favorite song of all time came through the speakers: U2's "Mysterious Ways." As soon as I heard those chunky chords at the song's opening, I wanted to hurl. It's a visceral reaction to the toxic stew of Bono's breathy vocals and the Edge's overly funky guitar. This song feels like I'm at Burning Man or something.

"Wait! I love this song. Turn it up!" he yelled. Then he shot out of bed totally stark naked and pushed me aside to get control of the dial. He inched the knob to the right, kicking it up a few notches, and seemed to delight in watching my face tense up.

I plugged my ears with my fingers in defiance. I narrowed my eyes. *I'm gonna kill him,* I thought. *I'm going to fucking kill him. I'll pull off one of his black socks and strangle him with it.*

He started singing along with Bono, swaying about three inches from my face. "Come on, sing along. I *know* you know the words." Then he moved his hands in a wobbly, psychedelic shape to go along with the music.

At first, I tried to laugh it off. "That's hilarious. Now, turn it off. I'm not even kidding."

Buoyed with finding my Achilles' heel in the U2 canon, he leaned in close to me and sang the next verse. All right, it kinda cracked me up to have a drunk, naked guy spewing U2 lyrics at me, but I couldn't laugh because I didn't want to encourage him. All I wanted out of life was to live in a "Mysterious Ways"-free universe. Is that too much to ask?

Finally, the song ended and he collapsed in the bed, like one of those animatronics animals you see at Chuck E. Cheese shutting down at the end of the show. I resumed my quest to find the worst song I could. I was downright determined.

"Come here. Come here, Sasha," he pleaded from under the covers. Getting seriously annoyed with me for taking so long, he started to make pouty, exasperated noises. There was no way I was going to sleep with this guy. The thought of waking up next to him seemed unimaginable. I'd rather be imprisoned in a third world country than kiss those lips again.

"Just a minute. I'm looking for the perfect song. Hold on." I settled on an eighties station that was playing "We Didn't Start the Fire" by Billy Joel, arguably one of the worst songs from the decade.

Never in my life had I wished so hard for someone to knock on a door. When I heard the telltale room service knock and the waiter's muffled announcement that our food was here, I bolted to let him in. When he wheeled the cart inside, I made a big fuss to let him know how greatly his presence in the room was appreciated. "Ah! Thank you, sir! This looks magnificent. Oh yes, right there is perfect."

I thought about scrawling a note on the bathroom mirror with my lipstick: "Help! A rich nerd is trying to cop a feel! Hand over the sandwich so I can be released from this prison." But I didn't do that. I thanked the man politely and devoured the food like that fucker owed me money. I don't think I even swallowed; I just pushed the food into my mouth. And, much to my horror, the sandwich was terrible. The roast beef was dry, the bread stale. The French fries were cold and rubbery. The side salad tasted like dirt. This was what I waited all night for?

Damn this sandwich and damn this stupid night! I clenched my fist and shook it at the sky.

"Sam, you want any of this?" I looked back over my shoulder. There was no visible movement from under the covers, but I did hear snoring. Not cute little kitten snores. They were huge, bellowing Santa snores. He made a chain-saw sound like a music box. An ambulance's siren would've been drowned out; that's how loud he was.

With my hunger sated and my eardrums assaulted, I knew it was time to leave. I tiptoed around his hotel room collecting my things. It was like I was trying to sneak out of my parents' house to go to a party on a school night.

That was when I spied two wrinkly dollar bills on his nightstand. Since I have impeccable judgment, I snatched them up and tucked them into my bra. He owed me at least that much for my trouble. (Mental note: Reimbursing me for my trouble is not expensive.) Then I got greedy.

I sneaked into his bathroom and scooped up all of the fancy toiletries, collecting the bottles in the front of my dress like a peasant harvesting foodstuffs. It was all coming with me: bergamot shower gel, citrus lavender body wash, vanilla mint mouthwash. Hell, I even tossed in a tiny pack of cotton swabs and a thin shower cap just for kicks.

I stuffed my dress full of the goods and surveyed the hotel room one last time, making sure I had all of my belongings. This had to be a clean getaway.

Certain I had everything I'd come with—purse, jean jacket, now-diminished pride—I gingerly closed the door. Then I sprinted down that corridor like an ax murderer was chasing me. The soaps and lotions jumped around in my dress.

Once I was in the elevator, I crammed my purse with the stolen swag. It looked like I had raided the travel aisle at Target. A full stomach, a full purse; the night wasn't a total waste.

Shielding my eyes, I walked across the lobby with my bulging handbag under my arm. The last thing I wanted to do was make eye contact with anyone. Naturally, I assumed the staff thought I was a low-end call girl because I'd stayed in this guy's hotel room for just under an hour. A small bar of hand soap fell out of my purse, but I didn't pick it up. I figured it was best to leave the fallen soldier and just keep walking so I kicked it under an overstuffed tan chair.

Outside, I jumped into the first available cab.

I didn't even hesitate. "Take me to the Sunoco on Twenty-fourth and Fairmount. Thanks." I directed him to a twenty-four-hour gas station/convenience store two blocks from my apartment. We were there in seven minutes flat. I got out of the cab and walked into the store, squinting as my eyes adjusted to the fluorescent overhead lights.

"Evening, ma'am," the guy behind the register said. I flashed him a smile.

"Hi, there." I pointed to the hot dogs slowly rotating in a roaster contraption to his left. "I'll take one of those, please."

Fuck sandwiches forever. I play on team hot dog from now on.

# CHAPTER 9

# I Am Impressed by the Worst Things Ever

I often think about what all of my conquests would look like if they lined up next to one another in a police lineup–type scenario. I already know the answer: It'd look like a clown college's graduation class picture, just a total freak show. Most of the guys would be under 5'8" and look like they hadn't showered in many moons. They'd be a mixture of dorks and misfits, awkwardly standing around like they were at a well-lit sixth grade dance. I think about my mother seeing the sorry lot of them, shaking her head and frowning, wondering where she went wrong.

"But, Mom, they're all great people." I'd point a few out. "That one knows a bartender who gets us free drinks. That one went to art school and now works at a video store. The one over there in the cardigan has a library card. You love the library!" That wouldn't make it any better. It'd probably make it worse.

From what I've observed, most women evaluate potential mates by the following criteria:

1. He must have a good job.
2. He must come from a good family.
3. He must have strong morals and values.

I seemed to have been absent that day in kindergarten when they taught this lesson, because those things aren't even in the top five for me. My top three qualities would look something like this:

1. He must have good hair.
2. He must have cool sneakers.
3. He must have an encyclopedic knowledge of the show *Arrested Development*.

Mostly, I'm impressed by things that shouldn't impress any woman, ever. For instance, I am impressed when a guy has Black Sabbath on his iPod. I'm impressed if he can toss food in the air and catch it in his mouth like a trained seal. I'm impressed if he can type at least five words upside down on a calculator, knows roughly seventy-five percent of the lyrics to Weezer's Blue Album, and has a prized collection of snow globes. Hell, I'm impressed if he's familiar with eighties sitcom theme songs. Now, if that's not a recipe for quality control in a mate, then I don't know what is.

There must be a flaw in my genetic evolution, because none of the attributes I admire in a man have a demonstrable advantage for me or my potential offspring. I've never heard of a woman being saved by a guy in the wild because he could recite the theme song from *Mr. Belvedere* on command or pop a blueberry in his mouth with his eyes closed.

I can see my future kids being pissed at me that I chose a guy to be their father solely because he played a song off the *Singles* soundtrack on the jukebox at a dive bar. They won't care how great the song "Chloe Dancer/Crown of Thorns" is; they'll scold me that I should've had higher standards. Point taken, future kids. Point taken.

I have been impressed by guys who can do high kicks like David Lee Roth, guys who know all the lyrics to "Bohemian Rhapsody," guys who can have entire conversations using only dialogue from Will Ferrell's movies, and guys who had a jean jacket in junior high school with heavy metal band logos scrawled in Sharpie all over it. Clearly, the bar to impress me is set woefully low.

Seeing as I have roughly the same interests as a preteen boy, it's no surprise that I'm impressed when guys get psyched about dinosaurs as much as I do. It quickens my pulse when he has a favorite dinosaur and can tell me why in a reasonably detailed manner.

I am impressed with guys who have deep voices. I've overlooked several obvious flaws in a guy just because he had a deep voice. Somehow hearing him say in his deep, manly baritone, "I keep pictures of me with my ex on my Facebook page because I like the way I look in them, not because I like looking at her," cushions the blow. If a guy could tell me about his favorite dinosaurs in a deep voice, I'd probably force him at gunpoint to Vegas for a quickie wedding with me.

Girls like to muse about the qualities their dream man will exhibit. Maybe he'll be a humanitarian, bringing light into dim huts in faraway lands. Maybe he'll be great with kids, rolling around in the dirt, mud stains on his Dockers be damned. Maybe he'll take Thai cooking classes, learn how to make his own compost pile, and/or take up yoga. These are all great things for a guy to do.

But I don't need a model citizen who pays his taxes on time and can speak three languages. My dream guy will hate someone for me on command. That would impress me. No argument, no reasons given; he will just hate someone because I hate him. And I do have my reasons for hating someone. They might be irrational or immature, but there are definitely reasons. And my dream man will accept it and share in my hatred, like a true love should. You know why? Because it's fun to hate people together. It's how we'll bond. Forget chocolates, flowers, and love letters. Screw sweet texts, blown kisses, and held hands. I know a man really loves me when he'll hate someone only because I hate that person, no questions asked.

Now, I'm the first one to admit that none of these traits—loving dinosaurs, having a deep voice, hating people for no reason—are particularly useful. They can't even be classified as skills, truthfully. But taken together, these qualities offer a composite of someone I'd like to do sexy things with and/or to. If this person walked into the room, I'd pull down my sunglasses to the tip of my nose and do a double take while I check him out like a bully in a John Hughes movie.

Recently, at a local Mexican restaurant, I asked Kat what impresses her in a guy. After wiping some salsa from her chin, she said with her mouth full of nachos, "Long hair and a bad attitude." She didn't even hesitate. It shouldn't have been a surprise; the girl has a serious boner for Nikki Sixx, Johnny Depp, and—get ready for this—Jesus. It makes sense if you think about it because Jesus was the ultimate long-haired badass, right? It doesn't take a session with Freud to figure out that her Catholic upbringing has influenced her attraction to the opposite sex.

"No! I mean what can a guy do that impresses you." I squeezed a lime into my beer can.

"Oh. Well, it impresses me when he has his shit together." Kat put her chip down at the edge of her plate. She was taking me seriously. "If his apartment is clean, I'm impressed. If he's nice to his mother, I'm impressed. That guy Riley FedEx'd me a dozen black leather roses that one time for Valentine's Day. I'm sure that required a Google search and a few phone calls, at least. That impressed me." She plunged a chip into a small dish of guacamole.

"Here's the thing," I said. "It's come to my attention recently that I'm impressed with, literally, the worst things in the world."

"Yeah, well, no shit. You pick, like, the *worst* dudes ever." If anyone could give a book report about the strange procession of dudes in my life, it'd be her.

"I know!" I launched into it, rattling off names like a camp roll call. "I went home with that Blake guy that one time because he was the same height as Michael J. Fox. That's one."

"Was that the one with the rocker haircut and the nice apartment?" she asked.

"Yeah, you mean the apartment that belonged *to his girlfriend* who was out of town? Yeah, that's the one."

"Didn't you also hook up with that guy at that house party just because you thought he was a dude in ZZ Top for Halloween?" Kat is like an elephant; she never forgets.

"Donnie? Yes. Shut up. That's two." Shit, I hadn't thought about him in a while. In fact, I actively tried to forget him. "You have to admit, it would have been a cool costume if that was actually his costume, which was never confirmed. I think he just had a gnarly beard so it was more of a costume coincidence." I kept going. "I also went home with that guy who reminded me of Riff-Raff from *Heathcliff*."

"The one with the puffy hat? And the bell bottoms? And the greasy hair?"

"*Yes!* That guy! I thought I could be his Cleo." It was a flimsy excuse, but it was true.

"But you don't own any leg warmers. Oh yeah, and you're not an animated cat from a cartoon that aired on network TV in 1985," she deadpanned.

"Well, that did not occur to me at the time. I blame tequila for that misstep. I also gave that one guy Tony my phone number just because he was wearing a Motorhead shirt and had an iPhone."

"I can't believe that impressed you. An iPhone? Really?"

"I mean, he must have a job if he has an iPhone, right? He can afford a data plan. What are they, like a hundred bucks a month? He's at least making a hundred dollars, minimum. It's reassuring," I said.

"Students have iPhones and they don't do shit." Kat had a point.

"I hooked up with that guy once who looked like Kirk Cameron. He turned that chair around and sat on it, just like how Mike Seaver used to do on *Growing Pains*. I went out with that guy who looked like David Spade and kept a knife on the dashboard of his car. I also went out with that guy down at the copy center that said that he could get me free copies if I ever needed any. I went out with the jazz piano player, the junior high music teacher, and the photographer who only took pictures of cats." I was running out of fingers to count on at this point.

"I remember that. Shit, you *are* impressed by the worst things ever."

"Dude, I know! That's what I'm saying. In my defense, Copy Shop Dude had the same hair as Tom Cruise in *Mission Impossible II*. It had some nice body to it. And sheen. He was like a stallion in a field, except instead of galloping, he'd stand still behind an enormous color copier."

Kat shook her head at me. I shrugged. I mean, what can you say with a track record like that? There's nothing to say.

The first time I remember being impressed by anything a boy did was when I was three years old. I met Christopher, a blond tyke who won my preschool heart because he told me that he could pee over his house. He might as well have told me that he could swim the English Channel after climbing Mt. Everest because my reaction would have been the same: total fucking awe.

He was my first boyfriend. We held hands and he'd show me how far he could pee, which seemed really far to me for some reason. I imagined him peeing with the force and pressure of a high-end Super Soaker. He could soak anyone if it came to it, protecting me with his golden stream. To this day, him showing off and tinkling on a small patch of grass behind my parents' house still ranks as one of my best dates of all time.

When I was ten, guys who could slide into baseball bases in gym class impressed me. As a chubby girl in high-waisted denim from Fashion Bug, I couldn't slide into shit. But I'd watch a guy just go for it, surrounded by a cloud of dirt like he'd just slammed a smoke bomb on the ground. He'd get up, dust himself off, and run across home base, high-fiving everyone like a maniac. I'd watch from the sidelines with my mouth agape.

This one neighborhood kid, Ronnie, told me that he'd attended a Milli Vanilli concert once, and I was enchanted. When he busted out the MC Hammer dance by the bus stop, I had to run home to take a cold shower. When a kid in my social studies class named Shane had four lines shaved into the side of his head and memorized all the words to "Ice Ice Baby," I fantasized about him for the rest of the school year. In seventh grade,

I fell for a kid named Jeremy because he was really good at doodling in his notebook during science class. You should've seen his doodles; they were next level.

By fourteen, I was impressed by guys who knew all the words to "Give It Away" by the Red Hot Chili Peppers. I was also impressed with guys who watched *120 Minutes* on MTV. While my classmates were slow dancing to "Stairway to Heaven" at the school dance, I was in the back of the gymnasium staring at the weird guy with stringy hair and a subscription to *Spin* magazine. My pickup line should've been, "Your beanbag chair or mine?" Sadly, I never got to use that gem because I didn't date any guys until high school.

I got into the local punk scene when I was sixteen and became impressed with even more esoteric, useless things: radical record collections, cool hoodies, and funny bumper stickers, to name a few. My first boyfriend had roughly thirty bumper stickers of his favorite bands plastered on the ass of his Ford station wagon. I thought it was awesome, even if it made him a magnet for cops. I could immediately identify his ride in a full parking lot at the mall; that impressed me! The fact that he had a well-respected zine made my knees go weak.

Moving to Philly didn't change my outlook at all. I once fell for a guy because he had a great white shark tattooed on his neck. I thought it was hot, even though I knew I could never take him home to my parents. There it was, thrashing up toward his ear with vibrant blues and greens swirling around the fins. I'd trace my finger over it and gently kiss it. I'd lick the skin and be surprised that it tasted like nothing.

Now, I'm stoked if a guy wears a cool hat, like the one Joey Jeremiah wore in *Degrassi Junior High*. I'm impressed with guys who look like they'd be in a barbershop quartet. I'm impressed if a guy went to a *Back to the Future* convention and touched a hoverboard.

Someone needs to shake me hard and set me straight. Maybe I can enroll in a VH1 show where I have to go to "Be Impressed with Cool Shit Boot Camp." Dr. Drew can analyze me in a group therapy session. I'll wear sweatpants, throw pillows at the staff, and cry on camera. At the end of it all, I'll be reformed and properly impressed with the kinds of things adults should be impressed with: robust stock portfolios, exotic dish sets from Crate & Barrel, and affordable cruises. Everybody wins.

I once kicked it with this one guy named Clark who was a total scumbag. Even though I'd had a crush on him for years, we were together only a short time—less than a week. Everyone knew he was a scumbag. Hell, even *he* knew he was a scumbag. He'd joke about it and say, "What can you do? I'm a bartender, for crying out loud! What did you expect?"

None of my friends could understand his appeal to me. I wouldn't even argue with them about it. "Yes, he's a jerk," I'd concede, "but he's so handsome." That was his get-out-of-jail-free card. Even though he was a scumbag, statistically, I think he impressed me the most out of anyone I'd ever met, and the reasons he impressed me were downright stupid. I'll get to that in a bit.

Sometimes you meet that one guy who just knocks you on your ass. Clark was that kind of guy. He was an ass-knocker, if you will. He was one of the first guys I met when I moved to Philly, and he loitered in my head for years. The first time I met him was at a dingy club called Silk City for a sixties soul dance party called the Turnaround. I was making my way through the crowd to the bar when he stepped in front of me, blocking my path. Before I could scoot past him, he leaned in and kissed me on the lips. It happened very quickly, before I had time to react. I let our lips touch for a second before I came to my senses. My first thought was that he had mistaken me for someone else.

"I'm sorry, do I know you?" I asked.

"Now you do. My name is Clark. What's your name?"

That's how I first met Clark. Kissing me was his pickup line. *Who does that?* No one does that. Clark does that. I took a step back and looked him up and down. At 5'6", he had a skeletal, bony frame and sharp cheekbones that would probably cut you if you approached him from the wrong angle.

You could tell that he had a particular style honed from years of patrolling thrift stores and specialty shops. He carried around old, dog-eared Bibles from the forties and Russian-English dictionaries in a weathered leather satchel. Basically, he looked like a homeless Civil War veteran. He should be warming his hands over a barrel on fire under a highway somewhere, chomping on a can of baked beans. And, as it turned out, he was the most handsome man I'd ever seen in my entire life.

"My name's Anna," I said.

"What are you doing after this?" he purred into my ear. I

couldn't breathe. Hell, I couldn't form a sentence if I wanted to. It was like the English language had escaped my brain. I was rendered mute in his presence.

"I don't know," I managed to stammer out. "I don't have any plans."

"You should go to the RUBA after this."

"The what?" I had no clue what he was talking about. "I have no clue what you're talking about."

"The RUBA. The Russian Ukrainian Boating Association? Ever heard of it?"

"The RUBA?" I repeated.

"It's a club around the corner." He did a little motion with his hand, like he was trying to show me what around the corner looked like. "I'll be there after this party. You should go."

"Okay. I'll see you there."

I had no clue what the hell he'd just said to me. I would later find out that the RUBA is an after-hours, members-only club tucked away on a side street that was open until four A.M. because it was privately owned and didn't have to conform to city laws that would otherwise make it close at two A.M. This was great news if you were the kind of person who had nowhere in particular to be the next day and could afford a late night with other restless souls.

"Excellent." He smiled, pleased.

I didn't go. I was pretty freaked out about meeting him, to be honest. The way he cold-stepped to me, the kiss, the telling me where to go: It was too intense for my brain. I needed to let

Clark sink in for a bit. I decided to leave it up to fate. If we were meant to be, I'd surely see him again.

I guess fate decided that Clark and I were meant to be—either that or Philly is just a ridiculously small town—because I ran into him four months later at a house party. Just as I was about to leave, he walked in looking like a fucking god in a brown leather jacket and perfect black jeans. I wanted to bite my knuckle like Lenny in *Laverne and Shirley* when I saw him walk into the house. I was stunned when he walked right up to me.

"Hello, Anna!" He remembered my name, and he seemed genuinely happy to see me.

"Hey, Clark, is it?" His eyes lit up.

"You remembered!" I sure did. We talked for a bit and, I'm going to be honest, I have no idea what I said to him. And as it turns out, the shyer I get around a guy, the more outlandish my nervous jokes become. The likelihood of referencing C-3PO, the *Naked Gun* trilogy, and/or a nineties *Saturday Night Live* character skyrockets. I probably should've had a huge cane pull me away like *Amateur Night at the Apollo*, but he was a good sport and struggled to put on a brave face even as I blurted out an unfunny *Wayne's World* joke.

After chatting for about twenty minutes, I told him that it was great running into him, but I was heading out. I had my car keys in my hand the whole time we talked, so it shouldn't have come as a surprise.

"Would you like a ride home?" I offered. Even though he

had just arrived at the party, he agreed to leave with me. I practically skipped to my car.

In that ten-minute car ride back to his place, I learned that:

*He went to Bible camp when he was younger.*
*He has asthma.*
*He was a communist in college.*
*He uses words like* rapscallion *and* buckaroo.
*He was once a merch dude for a popular rock band.*

To be clear, all of these facts impressed me. He was fascinating. I nodded along as we zipped through the Philly streets. As I pulled in front of his house, he handed me his phone number on a scrap of paper. Honestly, I'm thrilled anytime a cute guy wants my number, but watching him type my name into his phone is routine at this point. It doesn't feel special when I'm just a notch on his iPhone belt.

However, I love it when a guy takes the time to write his phone number down on a piece of paper and hands it to me. It's rad to empty my pockets at the end of the night and see his number folded up among my loose change and gum wrappers. And, it's fun to see his handwriting, even if it looks like he wrote his name while jumping on a trampoline. If it works out between us, then I'll tuck this piece of paper away in my shoebox of memories, where I keep all the rad things that guys have sent/mailed/made for me over the years. Yes, that slip of paper has the potential to make the shoebox cut; a sweet relic of our early courtship. I'm getting all glowy just thinking about it.

Then Clark kissed me again, this time a bit longer. It was just as gentle as before.

"We should totally hang out sometime," he said.

"Cool. I'd like that." I smiled.

"Well, I'm around. You know. Like, around. So, yeah. We'll talk soon!"

Wait, does he want to hang out with me? Maybe he doesn't? I'm perplexed! When a guy tells me that he's "around," I assume it means that he doesn't want to hang out. It seems like a squirrelly, noncommitted reply, right? He brought up the part about us hanging out, so why would he end on that nebulous note?

Where is this mythical place of "around"? Is it on the Internet, tucked away on a chat list? Is it in line at CVS when I'm buying deeply discounted Valentine's Day candy? Is it on the bar stool next to me when I'm out with another guy on a date? They aren't the same thing as scorin' some solo time.

As he got out of my car, he leaned into the open window on the passenger side. "I'd invite you in but my girlfriend is home."

"Girlfriend?"

"Yeah. You know." He flashed a smile. "So, if you call me and she answers, well, yeah, that's who it is."

"Oh." I told you Clark was a scumbag.

After he went inside his house, I crumpled up the paper he'd given me and tossed it into the gutter.

I'm telling you, Clark was a textbook study on being impressed by the worst things on the planet. I could see my family's reactions now if I brought him home for Shabbat dinner: My dad would ignore him, having no clue how to relate to him. My mom would wring her hands and silently pray that I didn't get pregnant by him. My little sister would text me from under the table, *Are you fucking serious about this guy???*

I backed off for a while, spurning his occasional advances when I'd see him around town. A few months later, on slick black bar stools under low red lights, he confessed that if he didn't have a girlfriend, he would pursue me in an instant. He said I was his dream girl, but he couldn't leave his woman. She would crumble, he said. I nodded like I understood, but I didn't. If he liked me so much, why wouldn't he want to be with me? He was bad news and I wasn't interested in a subscription.

After a while, he moved away to Austin, which was great. I thought he was gone for good and I honestly forgot all about him. So I was surprised to run into him at a dive bar one sunny May afternoon. He was sitting at the bar all by himself, reading a book.

"Clark?"

"Hey, Anna! How are you?" He put down his book and hugged me. "Sit down! Please, join me. What are you doing here?"

"I just popped in for a beer before I headed home. What are you doing here?"

"I'm just breezing through town. It's quite boring, actually. I have to renew my driver's license and pick up some things from my last job, so I figured I'd stop by the old stomping grounds for a few days. Let me get you a drink. What would you like?"

We caught up for a few hours. He told me all about his life

in Austin and how he was getting his act together. He seemed to be turning over new leaves left and right.

As we were talking, my least favorite bartender walked past us. I narrowed my eyes. "I hate her," I seethed. He spun around to get a good look.

"Well, I hate her, too, then. To hating her!" He raised his glass and we clinked.

"To hating her," I echoed. Then we both took a sip. He didn't even ask me why I hated her! My eyes sparkled at his ability to hate on command. All of those feelings I had for him came rushing back.

And our banter was off the charts! We were going tit for tat a mile a minute in a heated Ping-Pong match of conversation, like a zipper with two sides coming together seamlessly. Let me tell you, if there were a Boy Scout badge for excellent banter, he'd have earned it. He'd coach the younger Cub Scouts how to banter in specialty workshops across the tristate area. Really, it's a skill all guys should master, like tying different kinds of knots or shotgunning a can of beer. For a former high school debater such as myself, going toe to toe with this banter champion was pure bliss. Hands down, this was my favorite way to flirt.

"I'm staying at Franny and Chris's house for the next few days," he said.

"Well, you're welcome to stay with me at my place in Fairmount. Honestly, it would be my pleasure," I said.

"Really? It wouldn't be an imposition?"

"Not at all! In fact, I insist."

"Yeah, yeah. That'd be great."

"Okay, it's settled: You'll stay with me."

We took a cab back to my apartment, and I happily made us another round of drinks. The only thing I had in my house was some vodka, so we worked with that.

"Let's drink these on my roof. You must see the view. You'll love it."

"After you, my dear."

My heart fluttered a bit when he called me "dear." We climbed up onto my roof and sat down on the edge of the deck, so close together that our knees touched. The sky was a deep purple, like a melted grape Popsicle.

"Come here," he said as he tilted my chin toward his mouth. We had our first proper kiss under the winking sky.

"Hold on," I said as I raced back downstairs. I zipped over to the living room and grabbed an armful of blankets and pillows. As I popped back onto the roof, he helped me arrange the blankets so we could lie down and look up at the stars. Everything seemed perfect.

We got into a nice little rhythm with him staying at my place: I'd make us dinner, he'd pet my hair as we watched movies. We'd coordinate our schedules effortlessly, with him running errands during the day and showing up on my doorstep whenever was convenient for me. By the third day, it was almost like we were in a mini-relationship.

I learned so much about him those few days. For instance, I learned that he could do a crossword puzzle in one sitting. He zoomed through it with ease, stopping only every tenth clue to work out a tricky one, which he'd figure out in about ten seconds. I just sat there, amazed at his skill. When he finished, he'd read the lame punch line to the puzzle's theme out loud to me with satisfaction. Was there anything this guy couldn't do? It was even hotter that he filled it out in ink. That's some crossword cojones, right there. His crossword puzzle cocksure attitude impressed me.

I learned that his scars had good stories. One on his shoulder was from the time a guy pulled a knife on him (!!!!) during a rowdy house party. And another is from the time he lit his eyebrow on fire as a dare. I don't have any good stories to my scars. I once tripped by a swimming pool and have a nick on my knee. I also have a scar where a kitten bit me. *That's it!* Those are the lamest scars ever. I was totally fixated by his stories about his turbulent youth. It was hard to believe that this sweet guy was a teen troublemaker. How cute!

It turned out that Clark was the perfect movie-watching companion. This is important because besides going out for dinner, watching movies is one of the basic building blocks of a relationship. If dating were the periodic table, going to watch a movie together would be hydrogen (that's a science joke for all you nerds out there).

So you're in the dark snuggled up in a comfortable seat with a dude; what could go wrong? So many things could go wrong. Most guys get fussy and argue about everything. They have weird rules like they won't watch anything with subtitles or they won't watch anything they've already seen before or they won't watch something if I've already seen it.

But with Clark, I'd suggest watching one of my favorite movies, like *Breaking Away* or *Sid and Nancy*, and he'd happily agree. That's the thing; he was so open-minded about which movies we'd watch together. And he'd pay attention to the film I chose. He'd ask me to put it on pause while he took a bathroom break because he didn't want to miss one scene. We'd cuddle on my couch with his arm around me. He'd laugh at all the right places of the film. It was a downright pleasure watching movies with him! It made me sad to think about him leaving in a few days.

Of course nothing is that perfect. On the fifth day, the last day of his trip, I told him that I had a job interview the next morning, so I had to leave early. I let him know that he was welcome to stay and sleep in my bed while I was gone, which he said he appreciated.

Don't get too excited about the interview; the job was a long shot. It was for an administrative assistant position at a trade publication for medical equipment, and even though I had experience at magazines, I didn't have much experience with medical equipment; I'm sure using Q-Tips in my ears didn't qualify as medical equipment. But I was prepared to wake up early, don a gray suit, hop on a bus downtown, and make the case that I was the perfect person for the job.

I set my alarm for seven forty-five A.M. to be at the bus stop by eight thirty A.M. to be at my interview by nine A.M., my portfolio at my side. As I sat in the waiting room patiently until my name was called to see the supervisor, I got a text from Clark:

Come home now. It's an emergency.

Alarmed, I wrote back: What? I'm at my job interview across town.

Come home. Now. I think I need to go to the hospital.

I must've reread it at least three times. What could possibly have happened? Did he cut himself trying to slice a bagel? Did he sprain an ankle? What injuries could he have possibly sustained in my apartment alone? My mind raced with the possibilities.

What's the matter? I texted back.

Just come home.

Can it wait? I started to get very nervous. Then, the receptionist called my name, so I put my phone away and stood up to follow her. She led me into the supervisor's office and I shook the woman's hand, took a seat and tried to pretend that I wasn't totally freaking out.

I did my best to push Clark and his emergency out of my mind as I strained to make the case that I was a perfect fit for the job. I was a hard worker! And a quick learner! And, I cared about the medical trade publication world. (No, I didn't.) I bombed the interview. The supervisor even looked through my résumé and said that she had "no idea" why I was called in. Thanks, lady. She said that she would let me know what they decided in regard to filling the position, which was essentially a rejection.

When I finally left around ten A.M., I checked my phone and scanned through the seven urgent texts he'd sent: Please come home. Seriously, I think I need to go to the hospital. When will you be home? You get the gist.

On my way home, I wrote back.

Forty-five minutes later, I burst into my apartment, searching frantically for him. I expected to find his blood splashed across every wall in my apartment, dribbling down and staining my beige carpet. Would I get my security deposit back if there was blood on the walls? Wait, Clark was in trouble! There was no time to think about security deposits! He wasn't in my living room, my kitchen, or the bathroom, and there was no blood anywhere. He was in the last place I looked: on my bed, fully dressed.

"What's wrong? What's the matter?" I panted, frantically.

He looked up at the ceiling. "I think I'm dying. I need to go to the hospital."

"Okay. Why are you dying?"

"Just take me."

"Do you have health insurance?"

"No." He exhaled loudly.

"What are you dying of?"

"Alcohol withdrawal." He held out his hand. "See, I'm shaking."

"Let me get you some water." I kicked off my shoes and walked to the kitchen, where I saw an empty bottle of vodka sitting on the counter. He had finished the whole thing while I was at my interview. My panic was now replaced with anger.

I stomped back to my room and saw a glass by his side of the bed. I walked over and smelled it, whipping my head back when the alcohol hit my nose.

"How can you have withdrawal if you're drinking right now? That doesn't even make sense."

"I think I'm dying."

"You're not dying, Clark."

"Well, can you just come over here and snuggle with me? That'd make me feel better."

"I don't want to snuggle you, dude. You're acting insane! In fact, I think it'd be best if you leave."

"I can't leave, Anna. I'm dying."

"You're not dying! You're just drunk. You knew I was at a job interview."

"Oh yeah. How'd that go?"

"Terrible! I had a guy texting me that he had to go to the hospital the whole time."

"Oh, about that. I still think I have to go. Can you drive me?"

"Get out, Clark."

"I'm too sick to move. Give me two hours."

"Honestly, I think it'd be best if you left now."

"How about just one hour?"

"This isn't an auction! Get out!"

"Thirty minutes?"

"Okay, Clark. You can have thirty minutes. I'm going to leave now. When I come back, I don't want you here."

I kicked my dream man out of my apartment. As I walked outside and the sunshine hit my face and my stupid gray suit constricted around my waist, I felt like a little girl who wanted nothing more than a pony for her birthday. Then I felt like the girl who finally got a pony for her birthday and then realized that not only does it make a lot of noise, but it also takes huge, smelly shits on your floor and sends you bizarre text messages while you are out trying to get your life on track.

I thought Clark was my pony, but all I got was a jackass.

# CHAPTER 10

# Anna Goldfarb, Nerd Whisperer

Pro tip: If you want to know where all the smart, funny, nerdy dudes are, they're making the Internet. I wasn't always into tech dudes, but tech nerds have been going through a noticeable transformation the past few years. I don't know if they pooled their money together and hired a publicist or what, but tech dudes' dating stock has gone way up.

Tech guys are the new rock stars, except instead of sex, drugs, and rock 'n' roll, they wield unlimited data plans, robust RSS feeds, and strong opinions about Apple's business model. Podcasters are the new deejays. Bloggers are the new gonzo journalists. Online self-promoters are the new celebrities. Nerds are hot.

You know what cemented their status? The invention of the

iPhone. Like Samson with his famous flowing locks, guys who had an iPhone when it first came out were irresistible. What girl could resist: It was like they had two dicks and one of them had a touchscreen! Honestly, a touchscreen was cooler because it seemed like it was a magical toy sent from the future, something brought back from 2015 by Doc Brown in his flying DeLorean.

On the whole, we're talking about a pretty nerdy bunch of guys who jumped on the smartphone bandwagon when it first came on the scene in 2006. Frankly, they didn't seem properly equipped for the influx of female attention they received when they got their hands on those first iPhone models. They'd get nervous when girls approached them and asked to see their gadget. Some of the guys stuttered. Most of them blushed, their faces turning as red as a freshly spanked bottom.

Aside from their skittishness, which I find endearing in a weird way, I also like the way tech nerds dress. Hoodies and sneakers are a great look for any guy, which is great news because it's practically their uniform. They even make free T-shirts look good.

So, where does a girl who likes nerdy guys in hoodies, T-shirts, and new iPhones go to pick them up? Tech conferences, obviously. Just scanning the room at one of these events makes me want to give lap dances to any guy with a laptop, flash any guy with a flash drive, and install his Norton update into my Zip drive. It's downright unholy.

I attended one particular conference a few years ago to dip my toe in the local tech pool. It was creatively called the Philadelphia Web Conference, and it was crawling with hot nerds. There was one guy in particular who immediately caught my eye. According to the name tag slapped on his chest, his name was Patrick, and he was basically my dream man. With dark hair, glasses, and dark jeans, he looked like the sensible sidekick to a hip sixties spy. And, at 5'6", he was the perfect height for me.

Then I saw the hottest thing I'd seen the entire conference: As I studied Patrick typing away on his laptop, I spotted a flash of his pink argyle socks on his feet. Green and purple threads were woven throughout, giving his socks extra kick. Upon seeing him flash that diamond pattern, I had to hold on to the wall to steady myself. His socks knocked *my* socks off! He was basically wearing foot lingerie.

When he crossed his legs and exposed a good three more inches of pink sock, I wanted to hoot and holler while I tossed a stack of dollar bills at him. I've never been to a strip club, but if they had a bunch of chubby, short nerds writhing around in argyle socks, I'd be there every single night making it rain.

There is something about the kind of guy who wears argyle socks that makes me sit up and take notice. He probably has a library card, knows how to drive a stick shift car, and calls his grandmother at least once a week just to say hi. I'd even bet that he could sew a button onto a shirt in an emergency, has created at least one piece of artwork on his bedroom walls, and has a cool older brother. And it wouldn't surprise me if he owned a shoeshine kit and several seasons of witty British sitcoms on

DVD. This is the kind of guy that I saw myself with, my perfect other half in perfect argyle socks.

It was then that I decided that I wanted—nay—*had* to be the Firefox that turned his floppy disk hard. But I didn't want to spook him, so I had to move in slow, like an outdated version of Internet Explorer.

"Is this seat free?" I asked, patting the chair next to him.

Startled, he pushed his glasses up his nose with his finger and cleared his throat. His laptop shifted on his legs as he scooted over to make some extra room. "Sure, sure. Go right ahead."

"Hi! My name is Anna." I offered a friendly smile.

"Nice to meet you. My name is Patrick."

I pointed to his chest. "Yeah, your name tag told me that already." He looked down at the sticker affixed to his brown plaid shirt and let out a nervous laugh. "Yup. It's all true."

"Whatcha doing, Patrick? Seems like you're charging a lot of bullshit over there." I nodded toward the tower of power he had plugged into the wall.

"Oh, that? I'm just charging my laptop, digital camera, and work phone. Is that a lot? I guess it's a lot."

"I'm pretty sure that you're gonna drain the electrical grid for the entire East Coast. If we have a blackout in the next few minutes, I'm gonna blame it all on you." I smiled, but I don't think he saw because he turned his attention to the iPhone cradled in his hand. As this was the first iPhone I had ever seen up close, I was in awe.

"Oh, wow! Is that an iPhone? Can I see it?" I didn't wait for his answer; I let out a little squeal and immediately reached out for it, like a baby grabbing her favorite teddy bear from across the crib.

"Sure." He carefully handed it to me, like it was a family heirloom. He showed me how to swipe the screen with my fingers and zoom in and out with a pinching gesture. The phone was intuitive; it didn't take long for me to get the hang of it. I probably evolved into a higher life form just by touching the thing. I felt like the monkey wielding a femur bone in *2001: A Space Odyssey*. I wanted to hurl it in the air while beating my chest and letting out a primal shriek: What is this awesome tool? Arrrrrrrgh!

After watching me tinker with his prized toy for a few minutes, he started to get anxious. I frowned when he asked for it back.

"That was amazing." My cheeks were flushed. I could now understand the appeal of the device. I wondered if he'd notice if I stole it. I'm pretty sure he would. I tell ya, after holding his phone for 0.04 seconds, I felt like my shitty flip phone was a paper cup with a frayed string. No, wait. It was even worse than that. It made my shitty flip phone look like I was just cupping my hands over my mouth and shouting into the air. The damn thing was like a cat on its eighth life: It had been dropped on the sidewalk, used as a doorstop, and even doubled as a Ping-Pong paddle once during a particularly rowdy barbecue. They looked like they didn't even belong in the same category of electronics; like an Atari next to a Wii.

"I know. I waited in line for eight hours to get it." He rested it on his leg.

"I've never waited in line for anything. Well, that's not true. I waited in line for forty-five minutes once in high school to get Weezer tickets."

"Oh yeah?"

"Yeah. It was for their Blue Album tour."

"How was that?"

"Um, amazing. How was waiting for the iPhone?"

"It was a pretty nerdy scene. Like, it was probably better than the crowd waiting for *Star Wars* tickets; instead of dorks wearing shitty costumes jousting with cardboard tubes that were made into makeshift lightsabers, you had people sipping Starbucks and waiting quietly."

"So, there weren't any riots waiting in line for your iPhone?"

"Sadly, no. It was pretty civil. There was a lot of sitting calmly on portable chairs. That's probably the opposite of a riot, right?"

"Ha-ha. I guess. Was it worth the wait?" I asked.

"What do you think?" His turned the phone so the light reflected off the glass almost as if it was winking at me.

I chatted with Patrick for a bit and something became immediately clear: If NWA were the original gangstas, this guy was the original tech nerd. He was old school, a total tech trailblazer: He had a Twitter account before Ashton Kutcher typed his first tweet. He was on Facebook while the rest of the planet was busy customizing their glittery MySpace backgrounds. He had strong opinions about hashtag usage. Who had strong opinions on hashtags? *That guy did!* I was in HTMLove.

"What do you do?" I asked.

"I'm a social media specialist," he said. I'm going to be honest, I had no idea what that meant. Social media? I imagined a roomful of televisions having a tea party gossiping about the local townsfolk; not a viable way for an independent adult to earn a living.

"So, let me guess what you do all day: You check your e-mail, refill your coffee cup constantly, then dick around having meetings about how to integrate brands using Twitter and Facebook, right?" I joked.

"Yeah, pretty much. And, we have cake about once a week, too," he deadpanned.

"Cake makes everything better," I quipped.

"I would agree with that." He patted his belly. "Cake rules."

"No, seriously. What does a social media specialist do?"

He tried to explain his job responsibilities to me in detail, but he might as well have been explaining quantum physics in Swahili. Words like *product integration*, *assessment*, and *multiplatform coordination* were batted around. My eyes glazed over just typing that. His job seemed vaguely tied to Internet commerce. I nodded a lot as he rattled off a bunch of industry buzzwords. I think I looked like someone who understood what the hell he was talking about.

"I'm here to bone up on the latest social media trends and see what's blowing people's hair back these days," he explained. "Then, I take that information back to my clients and tailor integrated marketing campaigns for them."

"Well then, what's blowing people's hair back these days? I wanna be on the, uh, ground floor while I'm thinking outside the box."

His eyebrows arched up. "That was some impressive office lingo there."

"There's more where that came from. 'It's not rocket science that there's an elephant in the room. At the end of the day, we can't drop the ball. Let's run it up the flagpole and hit the ground running, but just don't screw the pooch.'" He clapped a little bit, which made me laugh.

"Thank you, thank you." I beamed.

"And why are you here?" he asked. "To lead a seminar on how to talk like a boss?"

"Actually, I'm here because I know the organizer, Rosie." The part that I didn't tell him was that she told me that these types of conferences were the best place to meet nice guys. Seeing as I had a lot of free time as a barely employed freelance writer, I figured I'd give it a shot. The fact that they had free lunch at this thing only cemented my decision to go.

"We should hang out sometime. I mean, would you wanna go out sometime?" He barely looked at me as he spoke. I could see beads of sweat forming near his forehead. He was literally sweating me.

My impressive display of cliché office lingo had charmed him.

"Totally. Yes. Let's do that."

"Are you around next week? We could grab lunch."

"Sure. That sounds great. Tuesday is good for me."

"Tuesday it is," he confirmed.

Yes, against my better judgment, I accepted his lunch date offer. Here's the thing: I hate lunch dates. They are the worst. For one thing, he'll be a stress mess. He'll show up panting 'cause he hoofed it the three blocks from his office to the restaurant. His shirt will be damp from sweat, so I'll have no idea what I'm supposed to do to greet him. An awkward hug? A kiss on his sweaty cheek? A fist bump? He needs to be doused with a bucket of ice water and a quick gulp of Gatorade, not embraced.

Second, he'll be distracted by the time constraint inherent in the lunch date format. Before we even sit down, he'll usually announce how he has only an hour to hang out. It's hard to be relaxed when he checks his chunky metal watch every five minutes to make sure he's not running late. We can't even enjoy the food because we'll have to scarf it down in order for him to get back to his office on time.

And, without fail, the first ten minutes of the date will be him just unloading about how awful his morning went. Yes, his boss was a total dick. How could the intern not know how to work a fax machine properly? Why is his secretary never at her desk? I'll nod, trying to empathize with his petty office dramas when what I'm really thinking is, *Where's the good-timey dude I met before and what have you done with him?* A lunch date dude is the exact opposite of the guy I want to share a meal with.

Plus, I'm going to be a terrible date. I'll strain to make small talk over a bento box lunch special. And, all my pretty clothes are nighttime clothes that show off my cleavage. What am I going to wear during a day date? A blouse? A T-shirt? It's all too normal for me. It'd be so much hotter with me in a low-cut black dress, tumblers of whiskey in our hands, and Velvet Underground on the jukebox. *Trust me on this.*

And the worst is that the last five minutes of the date will be him complaining about all the work he has to do once he gets back to the office. Great. I applied mascara for this complain-a-thon?

Then he'll ask me what I have planned for the rest of the day. As I'm a barely employed freelance writer, he'll be unimpressed with my answer of "grabbing iced coffee and sitting in the park."

That's when it will occur to him that our lifestyles are fundamentally incompatible. Disappointment will wash over his face as he realizes that I'm more of a free spirit than a fellow office drone; I don't wear business casual clothing or have adequate health insurance.

Lunch dates are a lose/lose proposition for us because I'll be annoyed at his khakis and he'll be annoyed at my loosey-goosey schedule. I guarantee that after he finds out about my aimlessness, he's not going to call his mom up and gush, "I found her, Mom! She's the one. Her name's Anna and she's a freelance writer who eats tacos, wears sweatpants until two P.M. on weekdays, and bats around catchphrases popularized by *Jersey Shore.* I know, I know; *it's just what I've always wanted!*"

I'm dreading it.

It's not worth hanging out with a crummier, stressed-out, slacks-wearing version of the dude I kicked it with just a few days ago. Let's save the dates for nighttime, where they belong.

Honestly, if I ever ran for political office, I'd ban day dates. It'd be the platform I'd run my campaign on. Just say no to lunch dating!

But I made an exception for Patrick because I liked him and I wanted to give him a shot. And, like throwing elaborate dinner parties and keeping your car's inspection sticker up to date, lunch dates are what responsible adults do. I wanted to act like an adult. So we exchanged business cards and he promised that he'd get in touch soon.

Of course, the first thing I did when I got home was Google him. I read his personal blog, which was mostly just funny YouTube videos and ruminations on marketing strategies. His Twitter didn't show anything juicy, just a lot of updates about his coffee consumption. I even found a jokey blog that he started with a friend two years prior but abandoned after a few months. It felt like rifling through his desk drawers or something.

Of course, I showed my mom everything that he had ever written. I'd follow her around with my laptop reading passages aloud while she did the dishes. She'd nod along and coo that he sounded like a great guy.

"Mom, he sounds better than great, he sounds amazing."

Then I showed his entire Internet presence to my two sisters and my best friends. I'd clutter their in-boxes with links to podcasts he'd done. It's like I was his publicist, talking him up by the water cooler: *Did you hear about this Patrick guy? He's a real mensch, that one.*

After everyone in my life read every word he'd ever published on the Internet, I downloaded a picture of him and made it my computer's screen saver because I'm mature and I don't jump into relationships headfirst before I really even know the guy. [*cough, cough*] Patrick was my dream guy. Now, all I needed to do was get to know him.

He didn't make me wait too long to plan our date, which I appreciated. He called me exactly two days after we met and we made plans to meet at noon the following Tuesday. I spent all morning getting ready. Seeing as this was a first date, I had to whip out the big guns: I shaved my legs and armpits, curled my hair into loose curls, and swiped on my lucky blush. For my outfit, I laced up my tan Pocahontas boots with the fringe on the sides and wore a loose blue dress. If I had to go through with this stupid lunch date, I was going to knock it out of the park.

I walked to meet him from my apartment in Fairmount down to Rittenhouse Square, a good twenty-minute stroll. As I turned the corner, I spotted him by the entrance of the restaurant nervously fidgeting with his phone. He saw me walking toward him and came over to greet me.

"Hey, there, Patrick!" He looked just as I remembered but a little more buttoned-up, not surprising as he came from work.

"Hey, Anna. You look great." As he took a second to look me over, his eyes hovered around my feet. "I love the boots."

"Aw, thanks." I looked at his dress shirt and khakis. "You look, well, you look ready to make a PowerPoint presentation." That came out wrong.

"It's the khakis, isn't it?" He looked down at his pants like they were an ugly birthmark he wanted surgically removed.

"No! They look good on you. You look fine. I mean, good.

You look good." What is wrong with me? Why the hell did I bring up his khakis? At least they were flat-front. Pleated khakis would have been unforgivable. I pointed toward an open table to quickly change the subject.

"Let's sit over there, by the window."

He swept his arm in front of him, put his head down, and said, "After you."

We made our way over to the table and sat down. I watched him look over the menu. He was still a little too shy to make eye contact, which I thought was cute. The direct sunlight illuminated a few wiry gray hairs on his head. There were more than I remembered, but I didn't mind them. Gray hairs equal maturity, so I was happy they showed up. I wiggled in my seat, pleased that I was on an adult date with an adult man for once.

Speaking of our date, things were going well. Yes, he did complain about his morning. And, yes, he did complain about the work he had to do when he got back, but he was good-natured about it. He wasn't too sweaty, which was great news, too. It was almost going too well, until he said the one phrase that had the potential to ruin the whole thing: "So, I Googled you."

I nearly spit out the sip of water I had just taken.

"Oh, really? What'd you find out? Anything scandalous? Did you find out about my love child with Richard Simmons? Or that I was a leader in an organization that hates J. Crew called the Crew Clux Clan? Did you see my spread in *Penthouse*? In my defense, I was young and I needed the money. Don't judge me," I joked. I was like a crazy person doing a verbal tap dance routine, trying to distract him from where the conversation was going.

What if he found out something super-embarrassing about me, like that I was the Wicked Witch in my eighth grade production of *The Wiz* or that I still have a Friendster account? (Confession: I haven't checked Friendster in more than four years and I totally forgot to delete it, but still, I have one.) Then, all the excitement about our first date would be replaced with concerns about my mental health because I still have an active Friendster account. (I swear, I'm going to delete it soon!)

I can't believe he Googled me! (Yeah, okay, so I Googled him, too, but I would never tell him about it.) If he *must* Google me, then please, for the love of all that is good and holy in this world, don't announce it as soon as there is a lull in our conversation. It's like admitting that he rifled through my trash. It's definitely *not hot* to watch him fly his stalker flag like that.

Thankfully, our food soon arrived, cutting him off before he could divulge what he'd learned about me by poking around on the Internet. I was thankful for that. But as soon as I placed the crisp white cloth napkin across my lap to dig in to lunch, I saw him take out his iPhone, point it at the food, and click a button. Hmmm. I rested my fork on the edge of my plate.

"Did you just take a picture of your roasted chicken?" I asked.

"Yeah." He was looking down, tapping his phone with his finger a few times. "In fact, I just tweeted it."

"Oh. Why?"

He shrugged. "It looks delicious. I figured my followers would get a kick out of seeing it." The phone buzzed, so he tapped it a few times, read the words that popped onto the screen, and laughed. "My friend George said that he loves the food here and that we should try the crème brûlée for dessert."

Okay. My boner for him was losing steam. It's bad enough that he's taking pictures of his food, but he's sharing them with all his Internet friends, *which is lame*! And rude. And just plain weird.

I guess I'm old-fashioned, but I expect when a guy is out on a date with me, it's just me and him—not his whole freakin' social network! C'mon, tuck the gadgets away, act like a big boy, and put the camera down. Disconnect from the Matrix for a sec and just enjoy the dish. I thought that he'd be more mature than this. Were his gray hairs a ruse? What's next? Is he going to write a Yelp review about this place before we get the bill?

For the rest of the meal, his eyes darted over to his phone to see if he had any new messages. I cleared my throat. I couldn't believe that I was competing for his attention with his gadgets. Sorry, touchscreen, I have breasts! Human breasts. Is that not good enough? He noticed me noticing his behavior.

"Oh, sorry," he said.

"No, it's okay." I tried to sound like I was unaffected.

"I should put this thing away, shouldn't I? Here." He popped the phone into his back pocket. "Is that better?"

I smiled. "Yes, that is better."

"Wait, what time is it?" he asked.

I glanced at my black plastic Swatch. "According to my watch, it's twelve forty-nine."

He picked up his napkin and wiped both sides of his mouth. "I should really get going. This has been fun. What are your plans for the weekend? Want to come over for dinner? I make a killer veal scaloppine."

"You do?"

"Not really. But I make pretty decent spaghetti. What do you say?"

I felt a little put on the spot, but I wanted to give him another chance. Gray hairs. Real job. His own place. I had to at least try a nighttime date with him. "Yeah, that sounds great."

"Terrific! Come over to my place Saturday night at, say, seven thirty. Cool? I'll e-mail you my address later." He was really sealing the deal here.

"All right, yeah. I'll bring over a bottle of wine. It'll be fun," I said, cheerfully.

He paid the bill and we walked out into the afternoon air. After giving me a quick hug, he left. As soon as he was out of sight, I whipped out my shitty non-iPhone and called Kat. I had told her about my date that morning, and she told me to call her as soon as it was over.

"So, how'd it go?" she asked, munching loudly in the receiver.

"Um, it was okay. What are you eating? That's like, the loudest thing ever." I held the phone a few inches from my ear.

"It's a carrot. I'm trying to be good and eat healthy this week. So, do you like him?" *Crunch crunch crunch.*

"He's fine. I think."

"What'd he do?" She sensed my hesitation.

"He tweeted a picture of his meal, like, in front of me."

"Yikes. Why'd he do that?"

"I don't know! It was pretty nerdy."

"But you like nerdy guys. You always do this, Anna: You say you love nerdy guys, but then you get one and you lose your boner for him because he'll do something textbook nerdy. You're racist against nerds. You're nerdist."

"I'm not nerdist."

"You are."

"I *love* nerds. No one loves nerds more than me." I was starting to get defensive. "But here's the thing: I thought he was a nerd, but I think he might actually be a geek."

"Oh, here we go. There's no difference between a geek and a nerd."

"There's a huge difference!" I protested. "Nerds are guys who are super-passionate about something. There's music nerds, art nerds, skateboard nerds; you name it. They have a level of expertise about a chosen subject. I'm a nerd."

"What kind of nerd are you?" she asked.

"I'm a nerd nerd! I'm nerdy for nerds."

"You're, like, the Nerd Whisperer."

"Yes! Exactly. I'm a Nerd Whisperer. But geeks? They have an element of social ineptitude to their personality. I thought Patrick was a tech nerd, but tweeting a picture of his lunch makes me think that he's a geek."

"Maybe he's a dork."

"Well, a dork is the kind of guy who's not just socially inept, but completely socially clueless. Like, Screech from *Saved by the Bell* was a dork. Urkel was a dork. I couldn't hang with a dork. Fuck no."

Kat munched on her carrots, absorbing my lesson. "So, how'd the date end?"

"He invited me over for dinner Saturday night."

"Huh. That's usually a third-date kind of thing."

"I know! I don't think he dates many girls, which is another check in the geek column. Honestly, he has no idea what he's doing."

"He's jumping through the date order all willy-nilly!"

"Totally willy-nilly," I agreed.

"Well, are you gonna go?"

"I already said yes."

"Well, you better not sleep over," she warned.

"I'm not going to. Don't worry."

"Promise me."

"Promise you? Are you serious?"

"Yes, I'm totally serious! You're gonna get overly nervous so you'll drink too much, then get too drunk and agree to stay over because you won't feel like going home. Don't do it! This is your chance to date how adults date. Don't blow it."

"That's not gonna happen. Patrick is husband material, not a bangmate. I don't think he's touched a woman this year, much less this decade. He's not that kind of guy. I'm not going to stay over on our second date. Besides, I'm treating this like an adult relationship, not a drunken hookup."

"Promise me!"

"He has gray hairs! I'm pretty sure he has an IRA! *He wears loafers!* This is the exact opposite of a drunken hookup!"

*"Promise me!"*

"Okay, okay. I promise you." Thankfully, she couldn't see me roll my eyes. Who is she, Mrs. Garrett from *The Facts of Life*? What's with the rules?

"Good." *Crunch crunch crunch.*

"Oh my God, those carrots! It's like having a chain saw in my ear. What are you up to right now?"

"I'm watching TV shows online, but my Internet keeps cutting out. So now I'm eating carrots and wishing it were a slice of Lorenzo's pizza instead."

"Good luck with that. I'm walking home."

"Okay. Have a good day."

"You, too."

"Don't stay over on your date."

*"Good-bye, Kat!"*

As I walked home, I thought about Patrick and our date. Fuck, maybe Kat had a point. I thought I was a Nerd Whisperer, but maybe I was nerdist deep down. The word rattled around my head.

The next few days, Patrick and I chatted online and gave each other little updates about our day. I learned that he is amazing at e-mailing me funny YouTube videos. Seriously, there are few things better than finding a guy who can tickle your funny bone via his keyboard. It is one hundred percent delightful. It's like having your own personal court jester showing up online to amuse you. I was warming up to him.

When his name popped up in the Gchat window blinking and pulsing, I'd eagerly click on the window to see what he had to say. People at the coffee shop would toss me dirty looks, as I'd almost pop a button laughing at his constant stream of entertainment. They were just jealous that I had a steady online comedy supplier.

When I had a frustrating day, after spending 1.2 minutes complaining about how my editor chopped up a story I turned in, this champ popped in a link to a website that played the sad trombone sound. Look at that: I'm smiling again! God, this guy rules. Kat was wrong. I wasn't a nerdist at all! I enjoyed his nerdiness; I was pro-nerd.

Saturday rolled around and I found myself standing outside Patrick's apartment with a bottle of cheap red wine. I splurged the extra five bucks and got the jumbo size—1.75 liters of liquid red gold. Not only were we about to have our second date, but it was also combined with seeing his apartment, which was a one-two punch of dating importance. I took a deep breath and rang the doorbell.

He came to the door and gave me a quick hug. "Why, hello there!"

"I brought wine." I held up the huge bottle as proof. He smiled.

"Here, I'll take that. Come in!" He took the bottle of wine and I followed him into his apartment. Immediately, I was punched in the face with a smell that could only be described as a locker room filled with rotten apples. I spotted a red candle in a jar set on his coffee table. Oh, that's his candle? He's trying to make his house smell like this on purpose? *Oy vey*. Who wants to smell spiced apples when it's practically summer? At least try to make your candle seasonally appropriate. Throw me a clean linen or sea breeze, dude!

Where did he get it? Maybe it was a present from a co-worker at last year's Christmas party. Who knows? I can't imagine him picking this thing out himself. Wait, let me picture it; there he is in Bed Bath & Beyond sniffing the lot of them, trying to find the perfect house candle. Oh hell, that's kind of cute.

And it's kind of cute to picture him fishing around for a match to light the thing before I came over. And it's kind of cute to picture him tilting the candle to light the wick, thinking, "Man, I am turning the romance in here up to eleven! This is really gonna set the mood."

Besides the noxious smell of the scented candle, I liked his place. It was warm and inviting. Belle and Sebastian softly played from his living room speakers. *Atlantic Monthly*, *Wired*, and *MacWorld* were fanned out on his glass coffee table. He had a real couch, not a shitty futon. I liked being there.

"Did you have any trouble finding my place?" he semi-shouted from the kitchen. I heard the pop of the wine cork as I looked at the book spines lined up on his bookshelf.

"Nope. The directions you gave me were spot-on." I was semi-shouting, too, but there was no need. I turned around and he was beside me with two glasses of wine.

"Here you go. What should we drink to?"

"Second dates?" I suggested.

"To second dates! Cheers!" We clinked glasses and took a sip. "Wanna see the rest of the place?"

"Yeah, give me the full tour."

"Okey-doke. Here's the living room." I nodded. "And this is the bathroom." He flicked on the bathroom light, shrugged, and then flicked it off. "That's not too exciting. And back there is my bedroom. It also doubles as my office."

"Do you mind if I check my e-mail real quickly? I'm waiting to hear back from my editor about a story I'm working on. Is that weird?"

"No, not at all! Go ahead. Knock yourself out. I'm gonna go check on the pasta. Come to the kitchen when you're done."

His room was very tidy. The bed was made. The table next to his bed was neat. Then I panned over to his desk. It was a straight-up shitshow. It was like he fed one computer after midnight and it reproduced smaller, more unruly computers. Let's back up a bit.

This is what I have, computerwise:

- one Mac laptop
- one power cord

This is what he had on his desk:

- two monitors
- two keyboards
- a desktop computer that he built himself
- a laptop that worked

- a laptop that didn't
- two sets of speakers
- a mouse
- external hard drives up the wazoo

Why does he need so many electronics? Is he trying to stop the Da Vinci virus like in *Hackers*? Is he trying to create the perfect woman like in *Weird Science*? Is he trying to fortify the compound during a hurricane like in *Jurassic Park*?

There wasn't even one square inch of free space on his desk to put my wineglass down, so I just held on to my glass and jostled his mouse to get his computer out of sleep mode. *Beep! Beep! Beep!* Oh, God, something started beeping. I was just trying to check my e-mail, and I accidentally set off a warhead! What kind of *WarGames* shit is this? Yikes!

The only good thing about his computer setup was that it had the most comfortable chair in his apartment. It had cushions on it. And wheels. And it spun. Besides that, everything about his computer area was dusty and complicated. The Borg had less wiring than his computer console. In fact, I was afraid to cross my legs because I thought I might dislodge some wires under there and inadvertently blow the entire thing up. I abandoned the effort of checking my e-mail and went to go find him on the other side of the apartment.

The table was set for two. He had a few lit candles in the middle of the table, which was kinda sweet. They helped set the mood. His spaghetti was fantastic and the music was good and sure enough, I got too drunk. The night was winding down and

I realized that I could either collect myself and call a cab or just stay put and enjoy my buzz with him.

"It's getting late. I should head out."

"You don't have to go. Stay over!" he offered.

"Nah. It's only our second date. I don't want to mess anything up."

"You're not going to mess anything up, I swear. Listen, you're drunk, it's late, just stay over. I want you to."

Shit, it did sound nice to just roll into his bed.

"Staaaaaay over," he pleaded.

"Okay. Sure. Why not?" I relented.

"Great!"

"In that case, I'll have more wine." I pushed my empty glass closer to him with two fingers.

"Now we're talkin'!"

As he topped off my wineglass, he said, "What time do you usually wake up? You're not gonna sleep in till two P.M., are you?"

"No, I'm not gonna sleep till two P.M.; I'm not a depressed teenager. Don't worry about it. I'll wake up whenever you wake up."

"'Cause I usually wake up early. Very early," he cautioned. "Usually, I wake up around seven A.M."

"On the weekend?"

"Well, yeah. My body is used to it. Is that gonna be a problem?"

I gulped. "No. That's fine."

Shit, seven A.M. was super-early for me. Hell, I didn't usually roll out of bed until *The View* started. I didn't realize that by agreeing to a sleepover I'd have to scoot out of his apartment at the ass-crack of dawn. Sheesh. What, does he have to wake up to tend to farm animals? Can't we just sleep in and get our snuggle on? Is lying around and giggling that unappealing to him? What's the rush?

But that wasn't my problem just yet. We drank the last of the wine and climbed into his bed. That was when he reached for the remote.

"Oh, hey. As a heads-up, I gotta sleep with the TV on."

"Whatever," I mumbled. I mean, what am I going to do? Argue with the guy? Technically, I was a guest in his house. In the interest of being a good sport, I agreed to give this TV thing a whirl.

However, I quickly came to regret that decision. As he was in deep sleep, I woke up in the middle of the night with the drone of infomercials zipping between my ears. No, I don't want to hear about the benefits of OxiClean right now. What the fuck time is it? Ugh. I hovered in and out of consciousness until the TV was just too much for me to take.

It became my mission in life to turn that TV off. I fumbled around in the dark, trying to find the appropriate remote controls. Oh, here's one. Wait, is it for the cable box or the television? I think I just turned the DVD player on. Fuuuuuuuck. I was basically in my own personal version of *The Hurt Locker*.

All I wanted was to stay over and snuggle this cute nerdy dude, but now I'm rummaging around his nightstand flicking various electronics on and off like an irritated zombie at Best

Buy. Thankfully, I managed to hit the right buttons and shut everything off. The room was silent. Finally.

Just as he'd told me, he woke up early and made a ton of noise. He opened dresser drawers and banged a few pots around making coffee. I rubbed my eyes and tossed my clothes on.

"Patrick, I'm gonna get going."

"You sure? You wanna grab brunch?"

"Dude, it's"—I checked my Swatch watch—"seven thirty A.M. No brunch places are even open yet. I'm just gonna head home."

"Okay. I'll call you later." He gave me a quick kiss as I headed out the door. Fuck. I slept over. Kat was going to be pissed at me.

"Dude, I stayed over."

"No!" Kat gasped.

"Yes, I did."

"Well, how was it?"

"Dinner was good. His house was nice."

"But?"

"But, he slept with the TV on."

"Oh, I *hate* that."

"Me too."

"And, he got up early. Like, super-early."

"You hate that."

"Dude, I know."

"Let me guess, you're over him."

"Well, I have a plan. I'm gonna have him stay at my place next time to avoid the whole TV-being-on-while-we-sleep thing."

"Okay. I'm sure that this will totally work." She chuckled.

"And I'm gonna hide the clocks so he won't know what time it is, to thwart the early-rising thing." I was pleased with my craftiness.

"You're gonna do a thwart attempt?"

"Yes, I'm gonna give him *one* more chance. I feel like he could be the one. This guy is, like, marriage material."

"You are ridiculous."

"This will work! Just you wait and see."

"Who talks like that? Are you a villain?"

"Yes. I'm the clock thwarter."

"That sounds like a medical condition. Not a good one."

I invited Patrick over to my place the following Friday. In preparation for his arrival, I stashed all the clocks in my house into my hall closet. My place was like Vegas: a clock-free zone. We were going to sleep late and in silence. There was no way for this to go wrong.

For dinner, I made him seared scallops and mushroom risotto. He finished his plate, which made me smile. Then we watched a movie because there wasn't much else to do in my apartment. As the night wound down, I invited him to stay over, which he eagerly accepted. As we drifted off to sleep in my silent room, I was pleased that I had both my quietude and my man.

So, I totally didn't see this coming.

"Where are you going? What time is it?" I rubbed my eyes. It appeared that Patrick was trying to leave my bedroom undetected.

"Oh, hey! I tried not to wake you but, yeah, I should really get going." He semi-whispered, darting around the room, fishing for his clothes that were scattered on the floor.

"Get going? Where do you have to be at"—I checked my nightstand, where my clock was noticeably absent—"what time is it?"

"It's six forty-seven," he whispered.

"How do you know the time?" I had hidden all the clocks!

"It's here, on my phone." He held up his iPhone and showed me the time on his home screen.

"Where are you going this early? Do you have a paper route or something?"

He finally stopped his scrambling and stood still. "I didn't want to tell you about this. Jeez, this is pretty embarrassing." He sat down on the edge of my bed and put a sock on. "I'm meeting my friends in Jersey."

"Okay." I propped myself up on my elbows. "That's not too embarrassing. Who's in Jersey? What are you going to do there this early on a weekend?"

"I really didn't want to tell you this."

Oh man. What was this guy about to tell me? Please don't let it be something Lifetime would make a movie about.

He took a deep breath. "I'm going to play Dungeons & Dragons with my friends. Go ahead and laugh. I know it's silly, but I've been playing with these guys for years. They expect me to be there. In fact, I'm already late."

"Let me get this straight. You're leaving a warm bed on a Saturday morning to go play Dungeons & Dragons? No, wait. You are leaving a warm bed *with a woman in it* to go play Dungeons & Dragons? Are you *that* interested in eating Doritos in a social setting? I think I have some in my cupboard; you're welcome to 'em."

"Well, when you say it like that, yeah, it sounds pretty crazy. But, I promised the guys I'd be there."

"This early?" He had to be kidding.

"Well, it starts at eight A.M. and we go all day. I was supposed to stop off and pick up snacks beforehand. Don't hate me." He checked his watch and his eyes bulged out when he realized how late he was. "I really should go."

He tossed his clothes on. His other sock was under my bed, so that held him up for a minute. He gave me a quick kiss on my cheek, then left.

The early-morning light hit my eyes like sharp knives. I collapsed back onto my bed and pulled my covers over my head. I just got ditched for a game of Dungeons & Dragons.

What a fucking dork.

# CHAPTER 11

# You Aren't My Ex

Looking over my life, I notice that I tend to get dumped a lot. If I had to put a number on how many times it's happened, I'd guess maybe a few dozen guys have pulled the trigger. I've never kept count. In fact, I do my best to forget about the dumping almost immediately after it happens. I just pretend it never happened. But now that I think about it, I've been dumped a ton of times. I don't know if I was born under a bad sign or I'm absolutely terrible at dating or what, but I'd say that I get dumped more than your average woman. Dumping me almost qualifies as a national pastime at this point. I'm talking, like, Jennifer Aniston levels of dumping.

And I get dumped all sorts of ways: by text, by phone, by e-mail. I've been dumped by letter, by him just fading me out and disappearing on me (that's called ghosting), and even by just suddenly changing his status to single online so I'm left to put the pieces together like an investigative journalist. Not to toot my own horn, but I think I'm good at getting dumped. I don't cry, I don't argue, I don't plead, and I don't beg. I take the news like a champ.

So, it was a strange thing for me to dump a guy for the first time. Guess how old I was when it happened? Fifteen? Nineteen? Twenty-one? Nope. I was twenty-eight the first time I properly dumped a guy. Twenty-eight. Let that sink in for a minute. Twenty-eight. I already had gray hairs sprouting on my head the first time I officially said "nope" to a suitor. I had already been legally driving a car for *twelve* years. I'd already voted in three presidential elections before I told a guy to buzz off.

Sure, I'd turned guys down before. I'd lost interest in casual flings and just ignored advances. But what I'm talking about here is realizing that a person is expecting to create a life with me and having to break the news that I didn't feel the same way. It was a big deal! I'd suffered several broken hearts over the years, so I knew that I was going to crush his soul. I had to come to terms with the fact that I'd be responsible for inflicting that kind of heartbreak on someone. It's a tough thing to rip out a guy's heart.

I didn't want to do it. My first instinct was to change my phone number, move to a new apartment, and drastically change my appearance like in *Sleeping with the Enemy*. But then I realized that I didn't feel like doing all that just to avoid an abrupt three-minute conversation.

I had some options to consider and some ground rules to set. I asked Kat to help me work out the dumping details. I promised her I'd make us strong-ass margaritas in an effort to sweeten the deal.

"Welcome to the official Dumper Directive Meeting." We clinked glasses and took a sip of our drinks.

"I hereby call our first meeting to order. First issue of the day: When should I do the dumping?"

"Soon. Definitely soon. The sooner the better. There's no point in leading him on."

"I know, you're right. It has to be soon. I agree. Next question: How should I do it? In person? Over the phone? By courier pigeon? What say you?"

"It has to be in person. That's the best way." Kat nodded, sipping her cocktail. "In person is classiest."

"Honestly, there's no way that I want to do this in person. I'm not cut out for that sort of thing. Can't I just send him a text? How terrible is that on a scale of one to—I don't know, what's something terrible?"

"Morning breath?"

"Morning breath is terrible. We'll go with that. So, on a scale of one to morning breath, how terrible is it to break up via text message?"

"Dude, it's beyond morning breath. It's dragon breath after eating a tub of garlic washed down with anchovies. You can't do that. Bucky is *in love* with you. Don't be a dick. You can't break up over text message."

"Kat, I know. But I can't do it in person. He'd probably cry.

His lip is going to at least get wobbly. I can't deal with that," I protested.

"Yeah, maybe the phone is better. He does seem like the kind of guy who'd cry. You're right, you're right. Phone it is."

"Okay, it's settled. I'll call him. What's the reason I'm going to give? How about, 'It's not you, it's me?'" I waited as she mulled it over for a few seconds.

"That's too cliché," Kat said. "You hate when guys say that to you."

"I do hate when guys say that to me, but it's not that far from the truth. It *is* me in the respect that I don't want to do any further dating."

Kat shook her head. "What else you got?"

"How about, 'I just don't see a future with you.'"

"That will crush him. You can't do that."

"How about, 'I don't want to waste your time.' That's good. It'll make it seem like I'm concerned about him and somehow this breakup will be in his best interest, too. I like it. I think that's the line to use."

"I'm lukewarm on it. What if you just said the truth?"

"The truth? The truth is that I don't think that I could ever fall in love with him." I took a gulp from my glass.

"Yikes. Don't say that."

"That's the truth."

"Just say, 'I don't see this working out. We're looking for different things.' The key is to be firm, but vague."

"Firm but vague," I repeated. "I can do that."

"Are you guys even a couple?"

"No! We've only been out twice. I'm not even technically his girlfriend, but he thinks I am."

"Double yikes."

"I know! He's falling hard quickly and I have to step up and break his heart. Fuck! You know, now that I think about it, I resent having to be the dumper here. All I wanted was to get a cuddle on and make out a bit, not ruin anyone's life."

"How are you ruining his life? Can't you just do the fade?"

"Nope. He wants me to meet his family next week. He's already told everyone in his life about me. He said that I was the best thing that's ever happened to him. I think he'll notice if I don't return his calls."

"Oh shit! He wants you to meet his family already? Yeah, you gotta dump him."

"I know. That's what I'm thinking."

"Cheers! To breaking hearts!" Kat raised her glass.

"I think I'm gonna puke."

How do you break up with a guy whom you aren't technically dating but who thinks that you are? We never had "the talk" saying that we were a couple. No online statuses were changed. He is a great guy, very handsome, too. But, I had to pull the plug.

Like most things, my relationship with Bucky started out as promising as ever. I had met a dude! He seemed cool! And then, we were going on our first date to a fancy restaurant that he picked out. However, as I waited for him to arrive, I had a minor issue: I had no idea what he looked like. I barely remembered meeting him and I certainly didn't remember giving him my number. I was pretty surprised that he called in the first place.

When he called to arrange our first date, I was in the middle of a nap, which just added to my confusion over his identity.

"Hey, Anna!" he squeaked over the phone. I tried to sound like I was awake, but I was severely disoriented. I have no idea why I didn't let this call go to voice mail, but for some reason I picked up.

"Hello? Who's this?" I said in my daze. My Caller ID had blinked with the name Nuvkt, which in retrospect was my drunken attempt to quickly type his name into my phone when we exchanged numbers the weekend before.

"It's me! Bucky!" he chirped.

"Who?" I rubbed my eyes. "What time is it?"

"Bucky! From the other night. Remember? You told me to call you. And, according to my watch here, it's five forty-seven P.M. Is this a good time to talk?"

"Yeah. Yes! Sure. I can talk." I was starting to wake up a bit. "Bucky. Right."

"You said, and I quote, 'You're totally gonna call me, right?'"

"I did?"

"You're hilarious! In fact, you made me promise you that I was gonna call. We pinky-swore on it. Ring any bells? So, here I am, calling. Just like I said I would."

"Okay. Hi, Bucky."

"How are you?"

"I'm good. You?"

"I've never been better. I just bought a new pair of shoes today. So, that went well. Good times. Good times."

I gritted my teeth. "Awesome."

I can't think of a more inane, grating filler expression than when a guy says "Good times" for no apparent reason. It's awkward and meaningless, much like our conversation. [*rimshot*] And he usually doesn't say the phrase just once; he'll repeat it a minimum of two times for extra effect. Guys who say it usually are known to buy gag gifts, wear shorts well into November, and heckle people from the away team at baseball games; they're horrible!

What can I say? I have an irrational hatred for this phrase. Is he wearing a What Would Dave Coulier Do? (WWDCD?) bracelet, because I'm pretty sure Dave would say "Good times" during a lull in his stand-up routine between his Popeye and Bullwinkle impressions. I don't want to date Dave Coulier and I don't want to hear him say this phrase to me. Ever. For anyone who chooses to say it, I have only two words: *Bad times.*

"Are you free Friday night for our first date?"

"You don't waste much time, do you, Bucky?"

"We already talked about this. Don't you remember? After you made me promise to call you, you made me promise that I'd take you out next week."

"I did?" I must've been wasted when this all went down.

"Is this the right girl? Anna? Tall? Brown hair? Big bazoongas? Hello!"

"Bazoongas? Ha! Is that even a word?"

"I think I heard it once in *Revenge of the Nerds*." That made me laugh.

"Okay. Where are you taking me for this first date?"

For some reason, I agreed to meet him there at that Mexican restaurant before it dawned on me that the only thing I knew about Bucky was that he was a male under forty. I had a feeling that he was cute, but I really couldn't explain why that feeling was there. I remembered thinking he was cute at one point during the night we met, but I didn't remember why he caught my eye. Maybe he had glasses? Or a beard? I wasn't sure.

Let's start with the things that I *did* remember about meeting him: I remembered dirty dancing with him behind a speaker at a club while the band played onstage. I remembered promising that we'd hang out soon. I remembered my friends waiting impatiently for me to say good-bye as the club was letting out. And, lastly, I remembered a general feeling of happiness washing over me when he kissed me before we parted ways.

Here's what I vaguely remembered about his appearance: He had dark hair, he was wearing a T-shirt, and he was definitely wearing shoes. Oh, and he had eyebrows. *That's it!* That's the composite I was working with. He could've been anyone with a pulse and a head of hair. That really narrowed things down.

As guys filed into the restaurant, I squinted my eyes, wondering which one was him. Wait, is that him? No, I think he was shorter. Is that him? Nah, he's too preppy. Honestly, I had no freakin' clue what Bucky looked like. I looked around the restaurant like a nervous squirrel.

Well, if there was any doubt about which guy was my date, when I saw him walk through the door, it all clicked into place. That guy must be my date. He had a huge grin from ear to ear.

"Anna!"

"Bucky!"

He leaned in and gave me a quick hug.

"You look great."

"Thank you. So do you." I looked him up and down and smiled.

Now I remembered him. Parts of the night flashed through my mind: I remembered him catching my attention as he walked past me on the way to the bathroom. I remembered liking his vintage Nike sneakers. I remembered grabbing his arm and saying, "Hey, have we met before? You look familiar." That was my go-to pickup line; it's an instant icebreaker.

I remembered him stopping for a second, then shaking his head no.

"What's your name?" I shouted over the loud music.

"Bucky."

"What is it? I thought you said Bucky."

"That is what I said. Bucky. My name's Bucky." He pointed at himself when he said it and stared at me. I remember laughing when he told me his name, because he did not look like a Bucky at all. His frail frame and pointy elbows were better suited to a name like Cullen or Seth; something introspective and delicate, like the kind of guy who'd keep a journal and wear thin cardigan sweaters.

No, Buckys are well-coordinated, masculine men who probably have several high scores recorded at area arcades and can throw baseballs with impressive accuracy. It was an overly masculine name for a petite man. It was almost comical how it didn't fit.

I knew right away that he probably didn't get a lot of girls because he was tensed up when I grabbed his arm. It was obvious that talking to women did not come naturally to him. It looked like he was having a meltdown and was about to blip an "Error! Error!" message as steam bellowed out of his ears. Unfortunately, I found his social ineptitude charming.

Long story short: I picked him up. Then I kissed him and made him pinky-promise that he was going to call me. Which he did.

We took our seats, and that was when I got a good look at him.

"So," he said.

"So." I nodded.

"It's nice to see you again!" he gushed.

"Yeah, totally."

"You look great. I love the dress."

"Thank you."

"I was so happy that you came up to me and introduced yourself. It made my night."

"Oh, wow. That's awesome, Bucky." He looked terrified trying to think of things to talk about, like he hadn't done his social studies homework and I was about to make him tell me what the ramifications of the Magna Carta were. He was more wound up than a Hot Wheels matchbox car as he strained to think of things to ask me. I watched him oscillate between stilted conversation attempts, straight-up conversation avoidance, and sheer terror. *I'm not an IRS agent performing an audit; I'm your freakin' date! Chillax!*

"Um, do you have any brothers or sisters or . . ."

"Yeah, I have two sisters. I'm the middle one."

"Cool, cool."

"So, Bucky. What do you do for a living?"

"Well, I could tell you, but then I'd have to kill you."

"No, really. What do you do?"

"I just said! I could tell you, but then I'd have to kill you." Then he shrugged his shoulders, like he was saying, *Hey, it's outta my hands, lady. That's the policy around here.*

I waited a full ten seconds to be dramatic. "Seriously. What is your job? What do you do all day? How do you pay your rent? Are you a can collector? Do you sell your blood? Do you sell vacuums door-to-door? What's with the secrecy? Just tell me!"

He was determined to stick to his line: "I already told you! I could tell you, but then I'd have to kill you!"

My face looked like he'd just told me that he had "only a handful" of DUIs or that he was really into the furry scene.

Well, he finally admitted that he works for the state government assessing whether businesses adhere to their discrimination policies. That's it? No Mafia connections? No spy work? Just a regular Joe with a desk job? All this hubbub for that? *Oy vey.*

As we looked over the menu, I noticed that his fingers looked like salted slugs that got smacked in the face with sandpaper. He appeared to be a chronic nail biter. Every time I looked over, he was chewing away on his middle finger like he was snapping into a Slim Jim. I'm sorry, but the only acceptable times to bite your nails are during a suspenseful scene in an action movie, if you are at the Oscars wearing a tux waiting to find out if you won the Academy Award for best director, or if you have a hangnail and aren't near an emery board. That's it! Those are the only times!

*Stop fiddling with your fingers. Put them away. Sit on them, if you must. Get a grip on something else besides your teeth.* Watching him nervously nibble on his cuticles while trying to have a conversation with me was beyond gross.

He looked really sweaty sitting there trying to think up things to talk about. I averted my eyes when he reached out to hand his menu to the waitress because his armpits had salad plate–sized sweat stains. It looked like his armpits had been crying. He needed to calm down. I thought about sprinkling a crushed-up Xanax on his mashed potatoes when he excused himself to go to the bathroom, but I felt like drugging him without his consent on a first date would be frowned upon.

For a split second, I wondered if this might be my fault. I flashed through a checklist: Did I have something in my teeth? Did I forget to put on deodorant? Is this dress on inside out? Did I mistakenly blurt out that I was going to perform oral surgery on him without anesthetic after dessert? Did I do anything to cause this extreme reaction?

Hell no, this isn't my fault! When he came back to his seat, he was shaking more than Sandy and Danny did in the Shake Shack (and that was a lot!). I decided that he needed a drink to, shall we say, unwind. I ordered us two shots of tequila.

"Here, this will calm your nerves." I pushed the drink toward him. "Just follow me: Lick the salt on your hand, take the shot, then finish with the lime. You ready?" He nodded yes. The shot went down smooth.

"Woo! There, that's much better."

"My whole body is tingling," he giggled.

"That just means that it's working."

"Let's do another one."

"You sure? Okay. Let's do another." We ordered another round, and it seemed to do the trick. Bucky was laughing his head off. And, as a bonus, his sweat stains appeared to have gone down roughly fifty percent.

"You're a terrific date, Anna."

"Oh, wow. Thanks!"

"I like you," he blurted out.

"Thanks, Bucky. I like you, too." This was the wrong thing to say. It just encouraged him.

"You know how this is going to go, don't you?"

"No. What are you talking about?"

"This. Us. How we're gonna go: On our first date, I'll take you out for a nice dinner. Done. You can check that off. On our second date, I'll make you dinner back at my place. On our third date, you can help me pick out a cat. On our fourth date, we'll go to Target and you can help me pick out some things for my living room. It needs a woman's touch. On our fifth date, we'll go to a pool party at my brother's house where I'll introduce you to my family. And, on our sixth date, we'll get married. Simple as that."

Bucky just did a love lockdown on me! I haven't even decided what I'm going to do in the next hour and he's already decided on our future children's names. In the time it took to do two shots, he's put a deposit down on our honeymoon vacation, listed me as his emergency contact at work, and tweaked his will to make sure that I am the sole inheritor of his prized baseball card collection. Talking to him is like watching the final montage sequence of *Six Feet Under* where we see how all the characters die. Slow down there, dude. His rush to lock me in as his future bride was giving me whiplash.

"You're kidding, right?"

"No! This is how it's totally going to play out. It's fate. Don't you think? If you hadn't said hi to me, none of this would be happening." It's flattering that he'd like to be legally bound to me in holy matrimony, but his zealousness rocketed from enchanting to alarming in record time. Oh, and I'm totally not helping him pick out a cat.

Our date went on from there. It was nothing to write home about. It was kind of forgettable, to be honest. We finished dinner and while we were waiting for our check, he told me that it was the best night of his life. I should've known something was up, but I pushed my reservations aside and tried my best to enjoy our time together.

I was on the fence because there were some good things about him. His manners were impeccable. When he asked me out again at the end of the night, I said sure. I figured I'd give him another shot. The fact that he worked up the courage to kiss me good night was admittedly sweet. Maybe the clunky marriage proposal was a tequila-induced fluke.

I invited him over the next week for dinner, and then we could have some drinks and go out dancing. He showed up looking like a British schoolboy in the sixties. Honestly, he looked good. Really good, which I was pleased to see. Dinner was fine; I made us fancy raviolis I'd picked up from Trader Joe's. He brought over a nice bottle of wine. Our second date was going pretty well. But when we got out to the club, he started slamming beers, one right after the other. I think the combination of second-date jitters and overall nerves got to him, because he got trashed.

"You think you should slow down there, bud?" I hinted.

"What? I'm fine. I'm better than fine. I'm amazing. I feel fantastic."

"Really? Because you look pretty hammered to me."

"Anna, I have something to tell you." He got very serious all of a sudden.

"Okay," I said, bracing myself.

"I think I'm falling in love with you."

"Bucky. You're drunk."

"I am drunk, but I'm also falling in love. You're the perfect girl. I mean, I love you!" He started laughing. "*I love you!* I want this whole room to know it. I don't even care. *I love Anna Goldfarb.*"

"You don't love me. You barely know me."

"I know that I love you. This is the best relationship I've ever had. You're my first girlfriend. Did you know that?"

I didn't say anything. I just watched him spin around the room like he was a nine-year-old boy who got a Nintendo for his birthday. He was going to be super-embarrassed tomorrow when I made fun of him for saying all that stuff to me.

That was when he started to cry. "I just, I just love you so much."

"All right, Bucky, I think it's time we left. Let's go home. You can stay at my place. I'll make you some food when we get back." I grabbed our coats and pushed him out the door.

I don't even know what happened. He'd shown up at my house looking like a million bucks. But through the magical powers of shotgunning cans of PBR and downing several shots of Jameson, he'd transformed himself into a blubbering mess. In the time it took me to sip my vodka soda with a twist of lime, he catapulted past the good-timey "lampshade on his head" party guy into drunk, slurring David Hasselhoff territory. He somehow managed to break his glasses on the dance floor, he gave the finger to the bouncer on the way out, and he smashed a party photographer's camera. After rolling around in traffic for ten minutes, he yelled at a cop and tossed a beer can at a passing car. Then he charmingly left his cell phone in the cab.

When we got back to my house, he knocked over my CD

tower and kicked over the coffee table, sending the nachos I'd just made flying onto the carpet.

And, as a shit cherry on top of my shitshow night, he stripped off all of his clothes and started puking in my toilet. Yes, I had a naked guy puking in my bathroom.

After a while, when the yakking subsided, I poked in to see if he was okay. He had his head resting on my toilet seat. "Get out of here! Don't look at me. I'm hideous," he wailed, his arms hugging the toilet bowl.

"Do you need anything? A glass of water? A stomach pump?"

He let out a low, guttural noise from the depths of his soul, the kind Chewbacca would make if you asked him to take out the trash while the Super Bowl was on.

"Ughhhhhh. I feel like I'm going to die," he moaned.

There wasn't much I could do for him. He passed out on the cold tile floor. In the middle of the night, I sneaked in and put a blanket on him. Poor Bucky.

In the morning, I made us breakfast and he emerged from the bathroom rubbing his head.

"Where are my glasses?"

"You smashed 'em."

"Where's my cell phone?"

"You left it in the cab."

"I'm so, so, so sorry for how I acted last night."

"You wiped out. It happens to the best of us. Here, have some breakfast." I pushed a plate of scrambled eggs toward him.

"You're the best girlfriend ever."

I didn't say anything; I just stood in the kitchen, mouthing the word *fuck*. I didn't want to be his girlfriend. What started as a casual hookup was getting too serious way too fast.

That was when it occurred to me that, holy shit, I was going to have to dump this guy. Sure, there were plenty of reasons to give him the boot from how he'd acted the two times we'd hung out, but it wasn't just one thing that made him unappealing; there were a lot of little reasons sprinkled in, too. I listed them in my head:

*He hates sushi even though he's only had it once.*
*He screamed like a girl at a cockroach we saw on the street.*
*He calls soccer "football."*
*He's never seen* The Wire.
*He constantly cracks his knuckles.*
*He is a loud chewer.*
*The fingernail on his pinky is a little too long.*
*He didn't know that the USSR doesn't exist anymore.*
*He texts me stupid shit at random times like* I'm bored *or* Thinking about making dinner.

After he had a few bites of the food, he cleared his throat. "By the way, I've already told my family about you and they can't wait to meet you."

"You did?"

He nodded. "I told them that I met my dream girl." He

grabbed my hand and kissed it. I gave him a half smile, then looked away.

Oh, lord. I had to dump him before this went any further. I hoped he'd just forget about having a crush on me. I tried to communicate this to him psychically by completely turning my face away when he tried to kiss me, but maybe he didn't pick up on it. I wished there were some document I could sign letting him know that I'm totally okay with him blowing me off, but alas, this wasn't the case. I was going to have to step up to the plate and dump him properly. I had never done this before. I was scared, so as soon as he left I called Kat for backup. That was when I promised her the margaritas.

I had settled on the line "I don't see this working out. We're looking for different things." Dialing his number was so hard. It was worse than doing my taxes. He sounded so happy to hear my voice, too.

"Hey, Anna!"

"Hey, Bucky. Do you have a minute? Is this a good time to talk?"

"Of course. I always have time for you."

I took a deep breath. "Listen, I don't see this working out. We're looking for different things."

"What do you mean? What are you saying?"

I stuck to my line. "I just don't see this working out. We're looking for different things."

"What? Why?"

"I'm sorry. I don't want to hurt you." He didn't say anything. But I heard his nose sniffling. Oh God! I had to wrap this up. "You take care now, okay?"

"Did I do something wrong? Whatever I did, I can change it."

"No! You didn't do anything wrong. You're going to make a woman very happy one day, I promise."

"I can't believe you're breaking up with me."

"Well, technically, we only went out twice. This isn't a breakup. Don't look at it like that."

"Wow, I went from having a girlfriend to having an ex in one day. I can't believe this."

"I'm not trying to split dating hairs here, but come on! This isn't a breakup. It's just, you know . . . a moving-on thing."

"You were my girlfriend. Of course this is a breakup, right? So you're not breaking up with me? Then why am I crying?"

"We've only been out twice, and for about twenty-five percent of the time we were together, you were puking! Take care, Bucky. I've gotta go. Good-bye." I hung up the phone. I'd just ripped his heart out of his chest. I needed a fucking beer.

I didn't see Bucky for several months. It wasn't until I ran into him at a party that things got weird: He introduced me as his ex to his new girlfriend.

It irritated me to watch him rewrite our dating history so flagrantly. Germany didn't win World War II, Mexico didn't land on the moon first, and I never thought of Bucky as my boyfriend. You can't mess with historical facts! What's next, is he going to tell me dinosaurs never existed? Or that *Gigli* was a good movie? It's madness!

I pulled him into a corner and hissed, "I'm sorry to break it to you, but, Bucky, you are not my ex. Do you know what the word *ex* means? It's shorthand for either *ex-boyfriend* or *ex-girlfriend.* You were never my boyfriend, and I certainly was never your girlfriend! We barely dated. We saw each other twice; that doesn't magically make me your ex-girlfriend."

"I don't know why you're being so difficult about this."

"I'm not your ex, Bucky. Just say that I'm your friend. If you *have* to communicate to someone that we went out in public together on two occasions, just say that we were seeing each other. Okay?"

He put his head down and walked back to his girl.

I'm not sure why he's so interested in being my ex anyway. There aren't any perks being in that club. It's not like he gets coupons to local establishments or a free sub at Subway. Really, it's no big whoop.

Now I run into him at the worst times. I'm not sure if he has some kind of premium iPhone app for showing up when I'd least like to see him, but without fail, he crash-lands on my fun planet at the stupidest possible second.

I'll be giggling up a storm with a dude I just met, and just when he takes my hand and asks me to dance, I'll see Bucky's face staring at me through the crowd, glaring at me all wounded like I just ran over his cat with my car.

Or I'll be yelling my phone number in another guy's ear and I'll look up to see Bucky leaning against a wall with his arms crossed, shaking his head. My new guy won't even notice it, but I'll feel Bucky's stony stare searing into my skull like a shitty laser. Why does he always have to magically appear when I try to get my swerve on? Did he affix a tracking tag under my skin when I wasn't looking? Is he a bloodhound, following my scent around the city? Sometimes, Philly just feels too small.

After a few months of his stare-a-thon antics, he worked up enough courage to come over to me.

"Hey, Anna! It's so great to see you." He leaned in to give me an awkward hug.

"Yeah! Hi, Bucky! You look well."

"Why, thank you. As do you. I saw you from across the room and so I wanted to come over and say hello. Gosh, can you believe that it's been two years since we went out?"

"I know. That's so weird."

"That girl I dated after you, she was just a rebound."

"How can there be a rebound? We never dated. We just hung out."

"What do you mean?"

"Bucky, you were never my boyfriend. That never happened."

"Anna!" He looked like I'd just knocked over his house with a wrecking ball. "How could you say that?"

"We saw each other," I clarified. "We were *seeing* each other, not dating." Basically, I'd just dumped him twice.

I finally walked away out of exasperation and went back to the table where my friends were sitting. Aislinn asked who I was talking to.

"Oh, he's just a guy that I was seeing."

"Is that why he's looking at you like he's going to cry?"

"Well, we dated for a week, like, two years ago."

"Only a week? It must've been some week. He looks like he just saw the first ten minutes of *Up* or something."

Compassion kicked in. I felt sorry for the guy.

"Fuck it. I guess you could say he's my ex. He's certainly campaigned hard enough for the spot."

# CHAPTER 12

# His Picture Lied

The whole point of the Internet is to make our lives more fun. Whoever invented online dating did not get that memo because, not to sound hyperbolic, but online dating is the worst thing that's ever happened to me. Let's just say that if online dating were a subject in high school, I'd fail it. I'd be forced to retake the class during summer school, but I'd fail that, too. The school would then threaten to withhold my diploma until I passed the damn class. And, after my third attempt at passing it, to the dismay of my friends and loved ones, I would drop out of school and get a job at an intersection selling bottles of chilled water on hot days.

On the whole, I'd say that my experience with online dating

has ranged from being mildly unpleasant to being downright terrifying (JDate, I'm looking at you). Maybe I hate it so much because I haven't found the right site for me. Like Goldilocks, I've tried almost every one out there and so far, none have been a good fit. I know it's possible to meet a good person through one of these sites; my older sister, Sarah, found her husband online. She tries to gently nudge me to give it a shot, saying that it worked for her, but every time I hunker down and try it out, I emerge with a mild case of PTSD.

All the guys on these sites look like pound puppies, with their little pictures and playful descriptions giving a quick snapshot of their personality. But instead of adopting my new best friend, dating online feels like interviewing a pool of wackadoos in a high-stress situation that leaves me questioning my attraction to the entire male species by the end of it.

Truthfully, I find the entire experience anxiety-inducing. It's worse than a dentist's visit or a tax audit. At least when I'm getting a root canal, I don't have to fill out an extensive application about my personal habits and partner preferences. Could you imagine telling your dentist what your biggest turnoffs are or telling Mr. Taxman what's the best lie you've ever told? That'd be hell!

Hands down, the worst part is filling out those online questionnaires. I hate coming up with witty answers about my interests. I have no patience for this part of the process. If I were an honest woman, I'd just say that I enjoy tweeting jokes during *Mad Men*, hanging out with my cat, Charlie, eating Mexican food, and quoting the dialogue to *Reality Bites* verbatim. Does any guy really wanna hear that? Or, more to the point, would any guy be attracted to that? No way.

Instead, I'll put something like, "I love my computer. And sleeping. But not sleeping with my computer. That'd be weird." See? I suck at this! I'd probably have better luck meeting my soul mate if I hired someone to fill it out for me. That is a service I'd pay good American money for.

Even if I made the most perfect profile with the cleverest, most perfect answers, it'd be all just to wander around a petting zoo filled with Kid Rock–looking hillbillies, uptight accountants, and divorced dads who can't spell very well. It's a significant time commitment to sort through the heap. At times, it can feel more like watching *American Idol* auditions than finding a suitable companion for sipping wine on a Friday night. It's like a sea of William Hungs overtakes my computer monitor when all I'm looking for is a Clay Aiken. (Talentwise, this metaphor holds.)

It doesn't help matters that I'm a grammar Nazi who takes great pleasure in overanalyzing minor spelling mistakes and grammatical oversights. I'm more than happy to jump to conclusions about his competency based on them. He was clearly raised in a barn because he confused *their* with *they're*. He can't figure out the difference between a possessive and a contraction? What a moron! There's nothing sexy about the process when I start bullying a guy's dating profile.

Occasionally, I'll strike gold and find a guy to double-click on. I'll scan his information like a pig unearthing truffles. Key words will pop out: *Ghostbusters*. Elliot Smith. *Rushmore*. "We could have a match here, folks!" I announce to an empty room.

Looking over his profile, I'll unleash a parade of exclamation points in my head: He's educated! He's funny! He drinks coffee! He has a job in a thriving field! Clearly, this man is my soul mate. We're going to have cute kids and dress them in little corduroy blazers if they're boys or cute, colorful frocks from boutique shops located in the upscale parts of town that have cafés with singer/songwriter CDs on constant rotation if they're girls. We'll pick cute names for them like Clementine, Ruby, or Simon.

I will have already imagined our life together and debated the best way to announce our engagement—Facebook relationship change or a tweet?—until I hover over his height and my smile will fade faster than Shaquille O'Neal's rapping career. At 6'3", he's too tall. It obviously wouldn't work out between us. *Next!*

Short guys are never honest about their height online because they assume that most women would be turned off by shorter dudes. I get that, but it makes finding my short prince that much harder. It's a first-world problem, sure, but it's still a problem. And no one seems to believe me when I mention in my profile that I'd prefer to date a dude between 5'5" and 5'10". Half of the inquiries I get are from tall guys arguing with me that I should give them a chance. I'm not interested in giving taller guys a chance; I'm interested in meeting my perfect short guy. I thought online dating was all about custom-ordering what kind of person I want to meet, not being attacked for my preferences. Frankly, I didn't come here to get confronted about this.

I also hate choosing a flirty screen name. I'll wrestle with this crucial element for hours on end, but no matter what I come up with, it'll end up sounding like a desperate, sugary soda shop concoction with an involuntary twitching problem: ClassicCoke-Winks, VanillaShakeShakes, PrettyPleaseWithACherryOnTop.

And I'm terrified about being matched up with a guy I've already dated in real life. With my luck, he'll be my first match. Oh great, the *one* guy in the city I never wanted to see again is now posing on my computer monitor doing something rugged in his profile picture, like hiking up a mountain or leaning against a Jeep door. It makes me wanna hurl seeing him in a Patagonia jacket and cargo shorts like he's filming a granola bar commercial.

I wish I could fill out a comment card on his profile to warn other women about his faults: "Jeff is a great guy—that is, if you like guys who have unusually long fingernails and whose snores sound like a chain saw making an announcement over a middle school's loudspeaker system." At least that would be some useful information on his profile *for once*!

I also can't stand reading boring e-mails. It's an unsettling experience to have semianonymous correspondence with people I have no interest in. I'm not here looking for unfunny pen pals, America. Of course I'll ignore the e-mails, which will just make me feel guilty. At first it was a thrill to get the attention, but that thrill quickly faded when I realized that I was getting fifteen e-mails a day from pale, nervous graduate students named Ben.

And, I'm going to sound like I'm whining here, but if by chance I do find a guy I like, writing witty e-mails about myself is exhausting. Who has the time to craft several in-depth e-mails detailing my personal and professional trajectory? Composing my college essay was less of a hassle. Can't I just say that I rule and leave it at that?

Every few months when there's nothing but reruns on TV, I'll have a spark of optimism and reenlist on a dating site. My first goal is to signal my availability to the right people. It's pretty simple:

1. I want to meet a short guy.
2. I want to meet the right kind of person.

I make sure to sprinkle in cultural clues to communicate my offbeat interests to the legions of potential suitors. I'll casually mention Apple products and my love of coffee, that's a given. I'll name-drop the Smiths and make an *Arrested Development* joke. For the bonus round, I'll even toss in a *Party Down* joke for the truly countercultural. In the minefield of online dating, those bits of information are essential to weeding out the duds.

However, it is apparent that most people on these sites lie about some crucial facts. Almost everyone tries to hide their obvious flaws, like that they are unemployed or that they still live with their parents. Even guys who declare that they are open books are lying about some aspect of their profile. It is impossible to tell the whole truth on an online dating profile. Maybe the way the picture is taken is hiding a receding hairline. Maybe he borrowed a friend's puppy for his profile pic to appear more approachable. There has to be something in there that is less than a hundred percent honest.

This isn't a terrible thing because truly, it's the mark of a sane person to fudge some facts. It's the ones who lay it all on the table that freak me out. When he types up his favorite sexual positions along with his sexual history in sharp detail on a public dating site, it makes me want to invent a time machine so I can go back in time five minutes before I saw his profile and toss my computer out my window, sparing me the trauma of glimpsing into his bizarre sex life. It's like watching Madonna's "Justify My Love" video: No one needs to see it. Not now or ever.

But what disturbs me most is that no matter how many online quizzes I take, there are still dozens of personality flaws that I cannot screen for. No online dating profile on the planet will prepare me for his chapped lips, bad breath, or terrible manners. Oh no, I don't get to find that out until he's sitting across the table asking to split the bill when the check comes.

For instance, online profiles can't screen for tumblers. You know, guys who bop around like life is one big Cirque du Soleil tryout. They'll use any excuse to kick out a cartwheel or roll out a somersault. As soon as their feet make contact with a patch of grass they'll bust out with a handspring or a round-off. I don't wanna date a guy who even knows what a round-off is! Guys like that always show off their flexibility. Like, they don't just touch their toes; they'll throw their whole body into it and bury their noses in their legs as they caress their calves. Watching guys bend in half like Gumby on four muscle relaxers doesn't do anything for me. I like my guys to fall head over heels for me metaphorically, not literally, so tumblers, acrobats, and gymnasts need not apply.

Or, what if he has floppy sleeve cuffs? Online profiles can't reliably screen for that. I'm not a fashion snob by any means, but if a guy shows up for our date with his shirt cuffs flapping in the wind like a dog's tongue on a hot day, I would probably zip around on my heels and pretend we never met. The only guys who dress like this are flashy magicians and eccentric millionaires on vacation and—news flash—I don't want to date either of them.

The only exception to this floppy cuff rule is if the year is 1992, your name is Eddie Vedder, and you're wearing a ratty flannel while you're filming a video for a song called "Evenflow." If that is the case, I might consider letting the open cuff rule slide. I didn't say I would, I said I might.

Or, what if his car smells weird? I definitely can't screen for this by scanning his profile page. What if when I open the passenger-side door of his car I get a whiff of the noxious air and it's like being smacked by the angry ghost of a McNugget? What if his rusty chariot smells like cat's breath mixed with a beer-stained, cigarette-burned couch cushion on a frat house's porch? Hell to the no.

I also can't screen for guys who wear thumb rings. They are the kinds of guys who worked on the student poetry magazine in high school. If, God forbid, I did date a thumb ringer, I'd have to prepare to have our entire relationship chronicled in some kind of art form. A comic, a short film, a novella, a painting—this guy must document everything that we do together. (Especially when I break up with him. That'll be his creative bread and butter for the next eight months, guaranteed.) A thumb ringer identifies with all of John Cusack's movie characters and looks to the stereo scene in *Say Anything* as the pinnacle of romantic gestures. When I try to dump him, he flat-out won't let me and will insist on several drawn-out phone conversations, asking me to go into detail about why I am unsatisfied with the relationship. Thumb ringers are the worst.

And I can't screen for guys who wear belly shirts. I don't want a front-row seat to his wiry belly hair convention. Eww. Unless he's ripped with washboard abs and he's playing a pickup football game with his buddies on a sunny day, there is *no reason* a grown man should wear a belly shirt. That little strip of tummy he flashes me when he reaches up to grab a cereal box on top of the fridge makes me cringe so hard that my eyebrows practically bend in half. I don't know if I should turn my head in horror or bust in with an armpit tickle to teach him a lesson.

Nervous tics, apartments that smell like cat litter, chronic knuckle crackers—who knows what weird quirks they'll exhibit? Clearly, I'm vulnerable to all of these horrible outcomes. Which online quiz can I take to weed them out? *None!* The answer is none.

Another possibility is that I'll meet a guy online, but he'll live far away. As a city dweller, I've made it a rule to never date a guy who lives in the suburbs. Sure, at first it sounds appealing that he is a homeowner and has a car—two things that can be rare with city guys—but everything else about his suburban living situation is unbelievably annoying.

For one thing, he will never know of any good restaurants downtown. I like it when my date exposes me to new places, but you can kiss that good-bye with a sheltered suburbanite. He only comes to the city once a month and when he does, he always goes to the same three bars. Consequently, I'll have to pick the places we go to on every date. This will get old fast.

And suburbanites will be overly concerned about where to park their car in my neighborhood and will ask me a minimum of five times if where they parked is "safe." Like clockwork, they will get lost easily on the "complicated" city streets. Hey, if you like giving directions over your cell phone to a panicky dude who took a wrong turn down the biggest, most well-marked street in town, then by all means, date a suburbanite.

Moreover, forget about going to their house for a date. Once I schlep forty-five minutes to his underdecorated condo, the panic sets in because it will dawn on me that we are in the middle of nowhere. When he explains that we will have to get in a car and drive to the nearest bar, I will frown. And when he whips out his GPS to drive to the restaurant for dinner, it will deflate any boner I might've had for him.

We can all agree that online dating is terrible and that dating a guy in the suburbs sucks donkey scrotum, but I've done it anyway. Like having a bat mitzvah, it's just something a Jewish girl has to do at a certain time in her life.

With a heavy heart, I pointed my browser to JDate, which would be a great site if I wanted to marry an overeducated, socially inept guy with clammy hands. After two days of being inundated by e-mails I had no intention of responding to, I canceled my membership faster than you could utter the words *matzo balls*. Online dating had been a bust. Again.

I waited a few months until I was vulnerable: I was bored, home alone on a rainy night. My friend Tia dates guys she meets online all the time, and she had recently met someone that she connected with. With a spark of optimism at her success story, I logged in to OkCupid and decided to roll the dice. Everyone says that OkCupid is the more "alternative" dating site, the go-to place to meet guys with record collections and sizable student loan debt. What better place to start?

After uploading three tasteful pictures of myself, I turned my attention to filling out my profile. I tried to signal my esoteric tastes by tossing in references to both Belle and Sebastian and Bruce Springsteen. I went with the screen name TwoCherry-Cokes and browsed the available men aged twenty-seven to thirty-four.

It was almost laughable how cliché the guys seemed. I saw video gamers who stared down the camera like it was trying to snatch their Mountain Dew and Ho-Hos away from them. Chill, World of Warcrafters! You're trying to get a date, not ransack my castle. (Is that even what happens in the game? I'm not sure. The only video games I've ever played are from the Mario Brothers franchise.) If we went out on a date, I would bet money that some form of fried chicken product would make an appearance at our meal, in either wing or finger form. I shuddered with disgust just thinking about it.

I also saw a lot of culture vultures hovering around. Their profile is filled with references to museums and symphonies, like they're the *Times* art section personified. They all know how to play the violin, are "great" at giving massages, and promise to indulge me in "fine dining" on our date. These guys are the update of the "candlelight dinners and long walks on the beach" suckers from way back when. They try to project an air of sophistication, but it comes off as cheesy and desperate. The only long, romantic walks I like are to the fridge or maybe to the corner bar.

If we were to go out, he'd present me with a lone, long-stemmed rose on our first date. I hate those things! Like, what am I supposed to do with it? Because of its stiff plastic sleeve, it won't fit in my purse and it'll just wilt over the course of the night like a corpse's finger. I'd also bet that he has a collection of sensual oils and lotions tucked away in a drawer by his bed that he'd whip out at the drop of a hat like a rogue Body Shop employee. Ewwww.

There's also a ton of deejays on there. They have a smattering of pictures of themselves sweaty behind the turntables, rocking out at a party. So he can twist knobs and score free drinks at a club downtown? Woohoo. (For the record, that was a sarcastic woohoo.) You can already tell that dating him will be a nightmare because deejays hook up with girls all the time. He sees drunken girls every week; how hard can it be? He's gotta bother us girls during the daytime while we're browsing the site on our lunch break with this deejay bullshit? Get outta here.

Then you have your sports fanatics, your hungry art students, and your pushy foreigners who constantly send inquiries. It's a madhouse.

After skipping them all, my mouse hovered over a cutie named NotoriouslyNice77. A port in the storm, his profile wasn't terrible. In fact, it made me laugh a bit. He said that he liked *The Big Lebowski*, the Pixies, and really good guacamole. I like all of those things, too. (To be fair, *everyone* likes the Pixies, but whatever.) Lookswise, he was good-looking. He seemed a little chubby, with dark hair and glasses with thin metal frames. His beard was full, which gave him a professorial air. And he had a sweet, Mona Lisa–ish half smile in his pictures, which I liked because sometimes guys can look too goofy with their huge, toothy grins. He seemed cool.

I investigated the second picture he had uploaded and my heart skipped a beat. If there was a hall of fame for profile pictures, I am certain that this one would be mounted on the wall, framed in gold. In his picture, the environment was warm and inviting. A soft yellow glow to the print, it was the picture equivalent of having a mug of apple cider on the first brisk autumn day. He was sitting cross-legged on the floor, sorting through a pile of CDs. I noticed Radiohead's *Kid A* on the top of the heap. It's like a *Where's Waldo* for hipsters.

He had a pair of headphones around his neck. Aside from a knit scarf, earphones are the only other hot neck accessory for a music nerd. Well played, NotoriouslyNice77. The plaid shirt he wore hinted at possible thrifting tendencies. I could hang with that. How much fun would it be to just lie around on a Sunday afternoon getting day drunk and watching movies with him? He probably knows all the best lines to *Point Break* and would totally call them out while we watched the movie together.

The one-two punch of eyeglasses and a beard was a home run. It's pretty much a foregone conclusion that he's going to be a hot dad in a few years. Could you imagine him with a Baby Björn strapped on his chest? This picture was like porn for secretaries who shop at Etsy stores during their lunch break.

I scanned his personal information and there it was, like a set of winning lotto numbers: He was 5'6". The sweet spot. He was the perfect height for me. I fired off a quick e-mail to him:

> Hey!
>
> I like your smile. Let's talk sometime.
>
> Smile smile smile,
> Anna

He wrote back instantly.

> Hey, there!
>
> Nice to meet you, Anna. That's a pretty name for a pretty girl.
> Are you around? Wanna chat?

Best,

Bryan

Sure enough, his little picture popped into a blinking chat window on the bottom of my screen. I eagerly accepted it.

We chatted for a few minutes and here's what I learned.

- He worked in a cable company and had lots of clients.
- He was a year older than me.
- He was having a good day so far.
- He thought I was cute.

So he had a job and thought I was good-looking. That's half the battle right there! I e-mailed him a few more pictures of me, and he did the same. In one, he wore a turtleneck sweater, which reinforced the professor thing. In another, blurrier one, he was jumping on a bed. I smiled. I like it when guys are playful like that. NotoriouslyNice77 was a veritable contender.

Over the next few days, we talked constantly. He'd text me cute things while he was at work. At night, he'd call me to ask how my day went and we'd chat for an hour, like we'd known each other forever. I began to think that maybe this could be my dream man. I tried not to get too carried away, but it became increasingly harder the closer we became.

He told me about how he attended Warped Tour in high school, and I thought, *Finally! A guy who could accept my love of mallpunk bands.* He told me about how he owns his own home, and I thought, *Finally! A guy who doesn't have any roommates*. He told me that he has a pet turtle and I said, "What kind of grown man has a turtle? That's weird."

"Spock's not weird," he said, slightly offended.

"You named your turtle Spock? That's even weirder." I had not planned for this. Maybe a dog named Spot or a cat named Fluffy. That's normal. But a turtle named Spock? I'm not the kind of woman who has turtles named Spock in her life. I'm just not. I crinkled my nose.

"He's so cute when he chomps on lettuce. You'll love him, I swear." Spoiler alert: I'm not going to love his turtle. Ever. As a lifelong reptile hater, I was sure of this. I shifted in my seat.

"Tell me more about your house," I asked, cheerfully.

"Well, it's a three-bedroom about thirty minutes outside the city. I need to fix it up some more. Right now, you can barely walk through it. There's a ton of boxes everywhere. I know, I should really put everything away. My mom keeps telling me that my place looks like a pigsty. Every time she comes over, she tries to make a dent in the mess, but she doesn't get very far. I'm always, like, 'Mom! Just leave it alone! I have a method to the madness,' but she doesn't listen. She just starts moving boxes around, standing in the middle of the room and shaking her head."

My mallpunky dream man had withered into a suburban hoarder mama's boy with a pet turtle. Gulp. I ignored these thoughts, figuring that I couldn't make a final decision about our compatibility until we met in person, which I still looked forward to. His house could be cleaned, his mother could be put in her place, his turtle could be released into the wild; these things are fixable, I reasoned. Besides, he liked *The Big Lebowski* and guacamole; there was still hope.

"Where should we go for our first date?" Bryan asked. "How about we grab a cup of coffee?"

Full disclosure: A coffee shop during the daytime is not my best dating arena. It's like having a gladiator fight in a tea garden; it's not the proper venue for the moves I wanna execute. Is this something he suggested we do because this is what adults are expected to do, like paying our bills online or throwing a dinner party?

I'm not sold on this coffee date idea because:

- I don't want to meet him somewhere well lit. We might as well have our first date in a dressing room at the Gap.

- Making small talk with a semi-stranger (i.e., him) while I'm sober just doesn't sound fun or sexy. Sorry.

- What if we hit it off? I'm not going to grab a second cup of coffee. If we went out for a drink, at least I could grab another beer seamlessly. I guess that's the point of meeting at a café—to limit our interaction time—but still, sometimes another beer goes a long way.

- If he talks my ear off, I'll have to sit there with an empty coffee cup pretending to listen as I get increasingly more jittery. I'm already nervous! Now, I'm nervous *and* jittery.

- How do I say good-bye to him? Do I give him a handshake? A high-five? A hug? A kiss on the cheek? I already know that we'll both have coffee breath. Eh. Count me out.

Couldn't we have just met up at a wine bar? Or a bar where he knows the bartender and can hook us up? To paraphrase James Van Der Beek in *Varsity Blues*, "I don't want your coffee date!"

"Why don't you come into the city and we can go somewhere around here?" I said.

"Sunday during the day is good for me. You?"

Hey, online dating is all about going out of your comfort zone, right? I gulped. "We could do brunch," I suggested. Normally, I would never agree to a brunch date, but my friend Lucy goes on a million Internet dates and she is a fan of the first-date brunch, if not the pioneer of them. She told me that brunch is the most low-stress, low-pressure meal of the week, so it creates the most relaxing atmosphere for a first date. "And, things are always better with maple syrup involved," she reasoned. I wasn't sure I agreed—my motto is "Things are always better with strong liquor involved"—but I was open to trying out this maple syrup theory.

"Yeah, brunch would be great," he agreed. "I have no idea where to get a good brunch in the city. I'm gonna leave that up to you." *I knew it!* Ugh! I hate when guys make me plan the date. I narrowed my eyes and gave him five demerit points in my head, like he was already in trouble with me before our date even started.

"I was thinking we could go to Silk City. Have you ever been there? It's a pretty great diner in Northern Liberties. Everyone loves it. You'll love it," I said.

"That sounds good. So, I'll swing by and pick you up at, say, eleven thirty?"

"You're gonna pick me up? Really?" I felt like Cinderella, being whisked to a ball where there would be plenty of maple syrup.

"This is our first date. Of course I'm going to pick you up. I'm a gentleman, Anna. What did you think, I was going to make you walk? What kinds of guys do you normally go out with? Do they not pick you up for dates? That's crazy!"

Whoa there, dude. I'm not sure how his act of chivalry turned into an attack on every other guy I've ever shared a meal with, but I felt a little defensive. "Well, usually I just meet guys at the restaurant for a first date. I am able to arrive at locations by myself. Shocking, I know."

"Well, that's not how I roll. You're a lady. You should be treated as such." For some reason, I felt like he'd said this line before. But it didn't matter. I played along.

"All right. But if you don't lay your cloak over a puddle for me, I'll be very disappointed."

"I'll be sure to bring it. There's no way that you'd step in a puddle on my watch."

"Yes, bring your cloak, for sure. I'll text you my address on Sunday morning before you head over. See you then. Oh wait! Is there anything I should know about you before we meet?"

"Like what?" He laughed.

"Like, are you a zombie? Are you a communist? Are you missing a limb? Do you have any children? Stuff like that."

"No, I'm not a zombie. I don't have any kids and I am not an active member of the Communist Party. Last time I checked, all my limbs were accounted for. Wait, is there anything that I should know about you?"

"I can't think of anything to tell you. I'm tall, but I've already told you that. Are you sure that you don't mind me being so much taller than you?"

"I've already told you: I don't mind at all. Seriously, I think it's cool. It'll be fine. It'll be better than fine; it'll be great. Awesome, even."

"Cool. How tall are you again?"

"I'm five-six. Well, more like five-five and a half."

"That's just perfect," I purred.

"Anything else?" he asked.

"Nah, I can't think of anything. Just make sure to smell good. And don't have chapped lips. If you do that, you're golden."

"Okay. I will smell good and I won't have chapped lips. Anything else?"

"I'm serious. Those are the top two things that most guys could do wrong in this situation." I couldn't tell if he was annoyed, but, hey, at least I laid it on the line. I was proud of myself for being so straightforward. Look at me, dating like an adult!

"Okay. Noted."

"It'll be fun. I'm looking forward to it." I smiled into the phone.

"Cool beans!" he chirped. I was confused for a second because *cool beans* is a phrase that should be used only by girls in 1997 writing yearbook inscriptions, not fully grown men talking to a potential date. You know which kinds of guys say the phrase *cool beans*? Drama club kids, guys who wear socks with sandals, religious missionaries, Dave Matthews Band fans, Hacky Sackers, and guys who own a turtle. Do you know what they have in common? They are all people that I would never date.

I didn't need a Magic 8 Ball to tell me that for our date the "outlook [was] not so good." But I agreed to it because I was trying to keep an open mind. And wasn't it my closed mind that had kept me single for so long, the reason I was in this situation to begin with? I took a deep breath. Bring the turtle owners on.

At exactly eleven thirty-five, Bryan's silver Mazda pulled up to my house. I bounded outside. He got out of his car to open my door when he saw me walking toward him and I gotta say, he seemed much shorter than 5'6". He must've been closer to 5'4", which, honestly, was too short for me. He missed my sweet spot by a few inches, which made me sour. To passersby, it must've looked like I was his babysitter or something.

I was too nervous to say anything; I just slid into my seat and looked around. The interior of his car looked like the Burger King's murder scene: There were fries under the seat, stiff from fast-food rigor mortis. Garbage was strewn everywhere and cracked cassette tapes lined the floor. Empty Coke cans were jammed in every crevice. It was like the inside of a meth addict's brain in there. He knew that he was picking me up for a date; couldn't he have at least cleared away the Big Mac wrappers and moldy coffee cups? Was he renting out his car as a bum motel? Is he morally opposed to air fresheners? What the fuck?

I watched him as he fastened his seat belt and, to my horror, he had dry lips. His pucker was scalier than a lizard's taint. I'm not sure if he was making out with sandpaper before he picked me up or if he'd used his lips to scrub his pots and pans or if he did some kind of extreme sport where he was exposed to dangerous elements, but his lips were disgusting. His lips basically had dandruff.

And the shit cherry on top of the shit sundae: He smelled bad, like he hadn't brushed his teeth in a week. I'm not sure if he willfully ignored my warnings or this smell was an improvement over his normal everyday stench, but I was livid.

If this date had an eject button, I would've pushed it. It's not like he needed to find plutonium to get us back to 1985; he just needed to *not* look like he'd been playing tongue hockey with gravel for the past four hours. ChapStick is available pretty much everywhere, so there was no excuse for this. I couldn't even look at him.

"It was easy to find your place. It's a nice neighborhood," he said.

"Thanks! Yeah, I love it." I looked out the window, wishing I could just jump out of the car and roll onto the sidewalk.

Then I heard a robotic woman's voice command us to "take a left on Spring Garden Street in twenty feet."

"Sorry, that's my GPS. I'll turn it down." A GPS? We're only going fifteen blocks in a straight line! I didn't say anything. I just nodded.

We arrived at the diner and he opened my door for me. It wasn't until we sat down at our table that I noticed he was missing a prominent tooth. I tried not to stare, but it was there: a black hole where a pearly white should've been. Missing a tooth is like the Snuggie of tooth troubles; basically, his smile was wearing Crocs.

What happened? Did he lose a bar fight? Did he run into a stop sign? Did he let it rot away without giving it proper attention? None of these scenarios made him look any more attractive. Should I pass a hat around the diner and raise the money for him to fix his mug? He's an adult man! Why is he missing a tooth? He looks like a bum fighter, for cryin' out loud. Then I had a flashback to his online photos and it made sense why he never smiled in any of his pictures. Fuck.

I had asked him on the phone if there was anything he wanted to tell me before I met him; did he not remember that he was missing a tooth? Did he not think that it was an important factoid to reveal? Is he so used to not having one that it's like wearing eyeglasses or having a receding hairline—an insignificant detail that he'd just absorbed into his being, unworthy of comment? I felt like I was on a *Hee Haw* audition.

And his shirt was too baggy for his body. Is he a juvenile

delinquent attending his great-aunt's funeral? Is he fourteen and interviewing for a part-time position as a shopping cart wrangler at the supermarket? There were *handfuls* of extra material surrounding every part of his torso. He looked like an inchworm in a sleeping bag. I hated his stupid baggy shirt. I felt like he might be trying to camouflage a potential moob situation. But honestly, I'd rather see a slight outline of a flabby moob than see several yards of extra fabric floating around his midsection like he's in a dream sequence. Seriously, a kindergarten class could huddle under this shirt on goof-off day in gym class—that's how excessively baggy that garment was.

Because I'm mature, I held the menu up high above my eye level so I wouldn't have to make eye contact with him for a minute. I needed to compose myself. *Just one meal and then you'll never have to see him again,* I thought.

"Does anything look good to you?" I said, my voice half-muffled by the towering menu.

"Yeah, totally. I'm debating between the pancakes and the waffles."

Thankfully, the waitress came to take our order. I asked for two poached eggs on rye toast.

"I'll have the pancakes. With a side of home fries. And a side of bacon. And a side of sausage, too. You know what? I'll have an English muffin as well. And two scrambled eggs. That'd be great. Thanks."

I'm not sure what kind of lumberjack competition he was training for, but that's a shit-ton of food. I wasn't even sure if it all would fit on our table. We handed our menus to the waitress, and I felt a pang of panic that my prop was taken away. I'd have to sustain eye contact with him now.

"You must be very hungry," I said, with a tight smile.

"Did I order too much? I wanted to try everything." He looked panicked, like he'd guessed the wrong answer on *Jeopardy!*

"No! It's fine. This place is great. I'm sure it'll be delicious." Why did I even bring it up? I'm terrible at this!

"So, we're finally meeting! I can't believe it."

"I know! Crazy, right? I can't believe we're in the same room," I agreed.

"There's something I should let you know, Anna. I'm not ready for anything serious right now. Since I just got out of a serious relationship, I've just been trying to go on a lot of dates and meet a lot of people. It's been going okay, but the more dates I go on, the more I realize that I need to just take things slow and really get to know the person before I jump into anything."

"Okay," I said, slowly.

"I wanted to put that out there before anything happens and this goes any further. You seem like a great girl, but I'm not ready to commit to anyone right now. I'm sure you understand."

I would rather listen to anything—an ambulance's siren, a seal's mating call, Fran Drescher's laugh, literally *anything*—than listen to this guy prattle on about where his head is at in regard to our blossoming relationship. Do you know why? Because *we've had only one date*. And it's gone on for only *twenty minutes*.

We haven't even received our food yet, much less entered into anything remotely resembling a relationship. Frankly, I resented the entire setup. I was a captive audience boxed into this restaurant booth. I had to make eye contact with him as he detailed every nuance about where/when/if/how he will be able to date me. Should I be taking notes? Will I be quizzed on any of this later? I felt like I was getting a book report on his emotions.

I guess it was cool that he wanted to be up-front, but this little prepared speech that he gave me was an insanely huge turnoff. I didn't appreciate his assuming that I wanted to be his girlfriend anyway. As Stephanie Tanner would say, "How rude!"

Besides the chapped lips and the smelly car and the missing tooth and the pet turtle, I wouldn't have wanted to date him anyway because he wasn't funny. He cracked me up a mile a minute online, but in person he was about as funny as a parking ticket—that is, not at all. When we first started talking, he was like the Old Faithful of humor; every time his name would pop up on my phone, I knew I'd be in for a smile. But the farther he got from the phone, the less funny he became, and that's the real tragedy here. (I also think that my local grocery store's not stocking Pudding Pops is a tragedy, just to give you some insight into how I classify tragedies.) How could he do that? How could he crack me up with his texts but turn out to be such a dud in person? What false advertising! What a bait and switch!

Between his unfunnyness, his extreme shortness, and his long-winded, unprompted relationship speech, I decided right then and there that he was off my buddy list.

The food came, and there was a quick rearranging of plates

to accommodate his feast. I nibbled on my toast as he shoveled a mountain of food into his mouth. We split the check, which was fine. I didn't want to feel like I owed him anything.

It was a quiet car ride back to my house, except for the GPS lady instructing us to keep going straight along Spring Garden Street. I let her direct him. In fact, I appreciated the break from the awkward silence. Plus, I was pretty sure that an old French fry on the floor of his car was now stuck under my boot, so I was focused on dislodging it without his noticing.

We pulled up to my street, and I pointed to where I wanted him to pull over. "Yeah, right here would be great. Thanks for driving. And thanks for coming into the city. I know it's a hassle for you."

"Oh, no hassle at all! In fact, it's been my pleasure." As he said the word *pleasure*, he leaned in and tried to kiss me. I say *tried* because his seat belt had other plans. Like a guardian angel made of woven fabric, it snapped him back to his seat with a thud. His seat belt was the hero of the date, like a bouncer who doesn't let guys dressed in shorts and sandals into the club: "Sorry, son. I don't see your name on the list. Now, get back in line!"

As he fiddled with his seat belt, I reached for the door handle, but I couldn't find it. My hand frantically searched the door for what seemed like an eternity until, at last, I found the latch.

"Okayhaveagooddaybye!" I tumbled out of his car, nearly slipping on that goddamn French fry. Once I was inside my house, I marched over to my computer. Lucy's maple syrup theory was bullshit. The only thing sweet about the day was deleting my stupid profile when I got home.

I haven't tried online dating since. Maybe I'm just better at dating in person. Or maybe I'm just terrible at accepting minor flaws in others. Or maybe I'm just terrible at dating in all formats, both digital and otherwise. That's probably the most likely scenario.

# CHAPTER 13

## Blizztarded

The news was calling the impending weather emergency a "Snowpocalypse," which sounded like the title of a Judas Priest album that I wasn't going to buy. The entire Northeast was about to be blanketed with a shit-ton of snow (roughly), and everyone seemed to be losing their minds. Weathermen were freaking out, calling it the "storm of the century." Supermarkets were hemorrhaging milk, eggs, and bread like the human race was about to become extinct and everyone somehow needed to make French toast to save their lives. Kids all across Philly were praying for a snow day, and it looked like they were going to get their wish. Every channel had panicky flashing graphics splashed across the television screen, like we all had front-row seats to *The Day After Tomorrow, Live!*

How was I going to cope with Snowpocalypse? Well, I

planned to flop around my parents' house in sweatpants and a hoodie, drinking several toasty mugs of hot cocoa. That was my emergency plan. The goal was to hunker down and avoid everyone and everything for the next few days as the snow did its thing. To be honest, I was looking forward to dropping out. I had several bags of marshmallows stored in the cupboard, so I was set on my end. Bring it on, Mother Nature. Hit me with your best shot.

The first few snowflakes had just started to fall when I received an instant message from Jack, a tall jock I'd gone out with a few times last fall. At 6'5", he was easily the tallest guy I'd ever gone out with, which made him an outlier, a fluke, an experiment gone awry. In an effort to broaden my horizons, I thought I'd give Jack a chance. Maybe I could overlook his long limbs and find love. Besides, I found his candor oddly charming. He was one of those guys who lays everything on the table, who says exactly what he's thinking when he thinks it. There was no filter with Jack. While at first that quality seemed refreshing, it became grating pretty quickly when he'd say blunt, strange, hurtful things. He had no tact, which was the reason he entertained me yet simultaneously repulsed me.

The fact that we even hooked up still boggled my mind. I mean, how could I take a guy like him seriously? He had a Sublime poster in his room under a black light that he'd installed himself. He owned several Hacky Sacks. Any of those things on their own should've sent me running. And they did. Until he'd pop up again like a persistent weed. Just from knowing him a year, I can say with confidence that he does a million terrible things all the time. He'd flake out on our plans at the last minute. He'd be a cheapskate. He'd argue about which movie we should watch. He'd invite his friends to come out with us even though I was looking to score some alone time with him. He'd agree to go to only two dive bars in the entire city, so every time we went out, we'd end up at one of those shitholes. Honestly, he was *the worst.* A total nightmare.

Consequently, I'd written him off more times than I could count. I deleted him from my Facebook friend list and I deleted his number from my phone (twice!). However, I've come to terms with the fact that it is impossible to hold a grudge against him. He's too wacky! And his tiny brain had a nasty habit of calculating the exact minute I would be vulnerable to his charms. Maybe I was getting over someone else, maybe I was just sitting around my room bored; whatever it was, he had an unbelievable talent for pouncing on me when I was most susceptible.

I hadn't talked to him in a few months, so I was surprised yet tickled to see his name blinking on my computer screen.

Jack: Yo. What are you doing for the snowstorm?

Anna: Hey, Jack. Uh, nothing. Why?

Jack: Come over.

Was this guy serious? We hadn't spoken in months and now he was demanding I leave my comfy couch to go see his tall, wacky ass?

Anna: Why? What's going on?

Anna: Did you just get dumped or something?

I didn't have to be Colonel Mustard from Clue to figure out this mystery; clearly Jack assumed that I was his backup. I'd have bet he thought I was just hanging out in his back pocket waiting to be called to service, like a reserve Marine or a gift card to California Pizza Kitchen. I guess I was flattered that he'd keep me in his Rolodex/black book/spank bank/rub club, but I had no idea why he'd keep me there. The few times we went out, his behavior was erratic and immature. For a split second I thought that maybe he'd grown up in the few months we'd spent apart, but those hopes were quickly dashed the more he typed away.

Jack: lol. You'd think that, right? 'Cause we haven't spoken in a while and I'm suddenly talking to you out of the blue.

Anna: Pretty much.

Jack: Come over.

Jack: We just got a wet bar at my house. It's fully stocked with whiskey, vodka, rum, gin—you name it. I'll hook you up!

Jack: Hello? Are you still there?

**Jack:** I don't even care. I'm just going to keep bothering you until you say yes.

**Jack:** Come over.

**Anna:** Really? You know if I come over to your place, you're gonna be stuck with me for, like, at least two days. The news is saying that it's going to be the storm of the century.

**Jack:** I know. Why do you think that I'm inviting you? I WANT YOU HERE.

**Jack:** You're totally considering it right now, aren't you?

**Jack:** COME OVER!

**Jack:** You can hang out with Suzy during the day while I get some work done from home. It'll be fun. COME OVER.

**Jack:** Two words: snowball fight.

**Jack:** Two more words: pillow fight.

I will say that the idea of hanging out with Suzy was a selling point. She's a good friend of mine and I hadn't seen her in a while. In fact, she was the one who introduced me to Jack during a block party last summer, as they were neighbors. He lived right across the street from her. At first I thought that she was dating him, because he came up to her and loudly smacked her ass while we were talking.

"Ow! Jack, knock it off," she scolded, while rubbing her backside. "Anna, this is Jack." He didn't even shake my hand, just nodded in my direction.

"What up, ladies? Fancy seeing you here."

"We live across the street from one another. Why wouldn't I see you here?"

After he left, I asked Suzy what his deal was.

"He's like my kid brother or something. He's annoying, he's crass, and he's loud. I have no idea how he gets so many girls. I will say this, though: He's got a good heart. Like, if anyone were to mess with me, Jack would be the first one out there cracking skulls. Besides that, he's harmless. Actually, he's a pretty funny guy once you get to know him." She shrugged.

Right off the bat, I thought Jack was a goofball so I didn't take him seriously. I couldn't take him seriously if I wanted to. Wearing ratty gym shorts, a Grateful Dead shirt, and a red bandanna tied around his head, he looked like a bum, like he would ask me if I had an extra quarter to buy a cheap beer down at the liquor store. There was nothing polished about him. It was clear by the way he sat on his stoop drinking a forty and chain-smoking that he did not give a fuck about anything. His hair was too shaggy, his attitude too lax. His shirt had a hole in the armpit and he had three tattoos that were Philadelphia sports team logos.

Like I said, he was also very tall. I don't notice tall guys generally, but apparently, I'd caught his eye. When he asked for my phone number at the end of the night, I thought he was kidding. I gave it to him anyway because I'm terrible at giving fake numbers. As the digits left my lips, the right ones kept coming out. When he repeated my number back to me to make sure it was correct, I reluctantly said yes.

"Here, I'm calling you right now so you'll have mine. When you save my name in your phone, save it as Jackass."

"Why?"

"'Cause it's funny! That's what everyone calls me."

"People call you Jackass on purpose?"

"You say it like it's a bad thing."

I figured I'd probably never hear from him again. So when he texted me a few hours later saying that he liked my bewbs and he wanted to take me out, I thought he was kidding as well. His jackassery was practically performance art, like Philly's own version of Borat. He was so uncouth, so unconcerned with saying and doing the right thing, it made me do a double take. Say what you will about his manners, but at the end of the day, he entertained me, which is what made me give him more attention than he deserved.

We made a few aborted attempts at dating, but it didn't go anywhere. We didn't work as a couple for a number of reasons: For one thing, he was six years younger than me, which got on my nerves. I know there's a cougar trend going on in society, but I have no idea why. Younger guys are the worst. He had no clue how the dating world worked. While he gave the appearance of wanting to do the standard dinner-and-drinks thing, as we came closer to our date, he did a total one-eighty, backtracking on the plans we'd made. Ultimately he rejected the idea of going out like well-adjusted adults. While initially he proposed grabbing dinner at a nice restaurant downtown, after a few scattered texts back and forth, he said that he wanted to hang out, watch a Phillies game, and grab Taco Bell for our first date. I'm serious! He was a classic date downgrader.

Don't get me wrong: I'm thrilled when any guy wants to hang out with me in public. I'm even more thrilled when he agrees to classify it as a date. I'm downright ecstatic when he makes a point of saying how he's going to take me to a great restaurant and then for fancy cocktails.

However, I am *not* thrilled when he downgrades our date in record time. What initially started as a firm offer to grab dinner and drinks tumbled into some loosey-goosey grab at makeshift plans. What happened? It was like watching the evolutionary chart in rewind; our date transformed at breakneck speed from a civilized, modern-day human to a slimy, prehistoric amoeba.

I told him I wasn't interested in grabbing Taco Bell for our first date, and he seemed surprised. The next week, he texted me that he had a better idea for our first date: He asked me to go with him to a Foo Fighters concert at the Waterfront in Camden. Apparently, he'd snapped up backstage passes through his friend and wanted to take me. I didn't care for the band, but the idea of grabbing free beers in a backstage environment sounded like a good time. The novelty of the experience won me over. I agreed to go with him. About an hour before we were supposed to meet, he texted me saying that he was unable to secure a plus-one after all, so would I "be cool" with picking him up after the concert and driving him back to the city where we could grab a drink together?

To reiterate, what started as an offer to buy me dinner and drinks had deteriorated into a request for me to drive by myself to Camden, New Jersey, and pick him up from a goddamn Foo Fighters concert. What, am I a taxi service now? Am I his mom in a minivan? Why on earth would I agree to do this as our first date? What the hell?

This type of date downgrade typically happens to me about once a year. It's like a teeth cleaning but even more unpleasant. So, when Jack pulled a date downgrade on me *twice*, I had no choice but to blow him off. He didn't take it well and hounded me for another chance. And, in a moment of weakness since I didn't have any other viable date prospects, I agreed to give him one more shot. He swore that he'd take me on a proper date this time. So we went out for a nice dinner, then to his favorite bar. It was pleasant. He combed his hair and shaved for our date. He said that he was so nervous to see me that he puked before I came over. I thought that was cute.

We were having a great time when, out of nowhere, he said, "You know, Anna, I think you should know that I'm a wild stallion. I can't be tied down right now."

What do you even say to that? "A stallion? Really?"

"I'm just saying that I'm not looking for a relationship anytime soon."

"Got it."

"I'm sowing some oats, living the life."

"Okay. I'm picking up what you're putting down, Jack."

"I just wanted to throw that out there, so we're on the same page and all. I don't want you thinking that this is more than just two people, going out, having a good time together, because I'm all about having a good time right now. "

"Message received, buddy. You're a wild stallion who needs his oats. Gotcha."

After that conversation, how could I possibly take him seriously? *He likened himself to a wild horse.* But here's the thing: It cracked me up that he would say that.

I thought he was out in the field getting his stallion thing on, so that was why I was surprised to hear him ask me to stay over, during a blizzard no less.

Jack: Three words: a romantic pillow fight.

Anna: That's four words.

Jack: Here's four words: Ana, come over already.

Anna: You spelled my name wrong. It's like, right there on your computer screen. And you got it wrong.

Jack: Two words: grammar Nazi.

**Jack:** Two more words: come over.

**Jack:** come overrrrrrrrr. I just got a jug of whiskey and I want you to help me drink it.

See what I mean? He makes me laugh. That's my Achilles' heel! I'll give any guy who makes me laugh a chance, even if he's a tall goofball jock who really should be shunned by anyone with ovaries.

I hate to admit this, but being stranded together with Jack in a snowstorm did sound sort of romantic. I pictured us in warm sweaters with deer and snowflakes knitted into cute patterns, cuddled up by a chateau fireplace like rich skiers in the eighties. I never got to ski in the eighties, and I certainly never got to be stranded with a guy in a chateau, so this might be the closest I'd ever come to living that dream! I had to do it. I owed it to myself to have a snow bunny snuggle. At the very least, I knew he would entertain me. It could be fun. I felt myself nudging toward saying yes.

**Anna:** Okay.

**Jack:** FUCK YES! This is gonna be awesome.

**Anna:** You're really fine with being stuck with me during a snowstorm?

**Jack:** I already said yes.

**Anna:** It's starting to snow.

**Jack:** Well, hurry the fuck up then.

Getting action with Jack was in my immediate future. I wanted to high-five myself for having a viable prospect. I tossed some clothes in a bag, lied and told my parents that I was going to a friend's house, then hit the road. Flurries came down light and fluffy, like God was shaking off his dandruff onto my windshield. I was genuinely excited that he'd have some kind of home bar setup. I thought, where on earth did this guy get a bar? Did he inherit it? Did he win it on *The Price Is Right*? Did he salvage it from a sidewalk sale? I pushed those questions aside and happily schlepped to his house through the snow with visions of exotic mixers dancing in my head.

Thirty minutes later, I arrived at his house, a tiny row house on a side street in West Philly. He opened the door and gave me a long hug. I will admit, it felt good to hug a taller guy. My head fit into his neck perfectly. Maybe this wouldn't be terrible. I set my things down on the floor.

"So where's this wet bar that you've been talkin' my ear off about?" I figured that the quicker whiskey showed up to this party, the quicker we'd get down to business.

I expected shticky barware and an array of shiny strainers and bottle openers. Maybe there'd be tiny, colorful umbrellas to perch on the rim. Maybe there'd be a wooden stool I could sit on so I could cross my legs and flash him a smile while he swirled a few martinis together. Maybe there'd be that novelty singing fish mounted on the wall like Tony Soprano had. Maybe there'd be a tiki cocktail mixer like Mrs. Robinson used in *The Graduate*. Frankly, I hoped he would have something a cool uncle would have, tucked in the corner of his living room.

"Right this way, m'lady." I followed him into his kitchen, where he bent down on one knee and swung the cupboard door open. It turned out that his "wet bar" was just a half dozen dusty bottles stashed under his sink. His motherfucking *sink*! This was no bar. I felt swindled with this bar description.

"Here it is!" he proclaimed boldly. My face couldn't hide my disappointment. *What a ruse!* "So, what's your poison? I can make whatever you want on the rocks. As a heads-up, everything will be on the rocks 'cause I don't have any mixers." Yup, laugh it up, Jack. The only bar here is my bar for dating guys without a bar, and I refuse to lower it. His "bar" got an F and we all know that spells BARF, which is frankly what I wanted to do when he asked if I wanted a drink from under his shitty sink.

"I don't know about you, but I'm gonna break into this whiskey. Do you want some or what?"

"Fine. I'll have some. With lots of ice," I said, dryly.

"That's gonna cost you extra. Just kidding." I didn't even recognize the brand of liquor he had. It was beyond bottom-shelf whiskey. It wasn't even a shelf, it was like it had been unearthed in a cellar buried next to Chester Copperpot's treasure maps.

"Cheers!" We clinked glasses and he gulped his drink down. He quickly poured himself another one.

"So, word on the street is that we're going to spend this snowstorm together," I purred.

"I know. That's why I asked you over here. That's the whole idea."

"So, what do you wanna do?" I looked around his small kitchen for inspiration.

"Wanna watch a movie?" He shrugged.

"Sure. Let me see what you have." As we stepped foot into his living room, I got a good look at his couch situation. And we did have a serious situation: He didn't have a couch. He had a futon. Whenever I walk into a guy's house and I see a futon, I let out a little whimper. I don't care how many pillows he tosses on the thing or how many blankets he drapes over the back, that uncomfortable piece of furniture will never be a couch. It's not even in the couch family. It's like a couch's second cousin's half brother's roommate. I'm pretty sure they're not even friends. If the couch got married to a sofa, the futon wouldn't even be on the invite list.

For one thing, we can't lie down on it comfortably together because it's kind of hard to be relaxed with a huge metal pipe digging into our backs. The pillows always slip through the arm railing thingy so we slide down like angel hair pasta through a colander. I hate that metal arm bar. Why didn't they make that out of something—oh, I don't know—*soft*? That one tweak would improve our time in his living room immensely.

I think a half-deflated air mattress has more cushioning than this futon did. It was all lumpy from years of flopping around, and it had weird stains on it that I don't even want to get into. *God forbid* if we ever got in a tickle fight and I somehow landed facedown on the fabric. I would do everything in my power not to inhale because I knew it would smell like pepperoni meets dog's breath. [*shudder*]

This futon had to go. It was basically going to be like trying to watch a movie while lounging on a barbecue grill with a cloth napkin on it. And that just made me sad. But I tried to overlook it and be a good sport.

I saw that he had an amazing, huge flatscreen television mounted to his wall. It was clearly the most valuable thing in his entire house. Guys like him always have the most amazing entertainment setups. Their entire house could be in shambles, nothing more than a pile of bricks shaped into a houselike formation, but the television set would sparkle like a JumboTron.

I scanned through his DVD stack and suggested we watch *The Big Lebowski* or *Back to the Future*, but he wasn't interested.

"Have you ever seen this?" That's when he pulled out *The Endless Summer* from the stack and tossed it at me. It was a surfing movie that came out in the sixties. "Come on! Give it a chance." I shrugged and said okay.

Not to brag, but I think it was pretty awesome of me to indulge his request to watch a movie about surfing when I have zero interest in the subject matter. *The Endless Summer*, *Step into Liquid*, *Riding Giants*: I've seen them all. Like I give a shit about some dude surfing a wave.

Sure, I'll even pretend to get a little upset when some famous surfer dies after an epic wipeout. Boo-hoo. Huge waves can be dangerous: I got the memo, every single surfing movie out there! Mother Nature can be a cruel bitch, and surfers walk the line every time they go out into the ocean; got it.

Good luck finding a girl to tolerate a more boring genre of film. I didn't roll my eyes, cross my arms, and huff loudly after two hours of monotone narration spoken over repetitive footage of waves. Not me! I played along and marveled at the rip curls. What girl gives a fuck about rip curls? None! All I'm saying is that it's something about me to appreciate.

As we tried to curl up on his futon, that was when I noticed how drafty it was in there. My teeth started chattering and I could practically see my breath when I exhaled. If I listened hard, I was pretty sure that I could hear the wind rushing in through the cracks around the windowsills. *Why is it so cold in here?*

I get that he's trying to keep his heating costs down, but couldn't he get his Home Depot on and affix plastic sheeting around those drafty windows? Throw me a winter-preparedness bone here! A rubber glove would've provided more insulation than these flimsy, drafty windows. Were they made of Saran Wrap? I considered stripping down and flinging myself into a long, hot shower to warm up, but the thought of having to exist in his freezing house with wet skin made me want to cash out my paltry 401(k) and buy a one-way ticket to somewhere tropical like in *How Stella Got Her Groove Back*. (I've never watched the movie, but I imagine that a guy's cold house might have been a component to the plot.)

I'm like Raymond BURRRRRR in *Perry Mason*. I own a horse named Mr. Ed and my name is WilBURRRRRR! I'm John Travolta in *Saturday Night Fever* and I'm dancing to the song "BURRRRRRn, Baby, BURRRRRRn."

"Seriously, Jack. I'm freezing here."

"Just come closer. Let's warm up with some body heat."

"Aren't you freezing, too?"

"No way. The whiskey is warming me up. You want some more? I'm gonna grab some."

"Nah. I'm good." Jack proceeded to get trashed, downing whiskey like it was Kool-Aid. After a while, the whiskey coupled with the boring movie knocked him out.

"Jack? Jack. Wake up." He didn't move. He started snoring.

Fuck it. I wasn't going to get any action. He was dead to the world. I left him on the futon and ventured upstairs to find his bedroom.

I popped into the bathroom and I gasped. It was a total guy's bathroom. His shower was cluttered with an array of products with no more than a quarter inch of shampoo left in each of the crusty, dank plastic bottles. They were propped up on the edge of the tub like a police lineup. He had the usual suspects: White Rain, Suave, VO5, Fructis, and Selsun Blue.

I'm not a shampoo snob—well, maybe I am—but I'd rather use plain water than lather up with anything in this moldy shampoo graveyard. He doesn't have to be a metrosexual Aveda freak, but a little bit of a higher-end shampoo would've gone a long way.

He had one cracked bar of plain white soap by the sink that made me feel like I was sudsing up in a prison. Of course the rusty faucet only let about two drops of water cascade down at a time, so trying to wash my hands took way too long. And the only thing he had for facewash was a nearly spent tube of St.

Ives Apricot Scrub. That stuff makes me feel like I'm washing my face with gravel. I wasn't interested in any of this.

When I went to dry off my hands, there weren't any towels to be found. I reached for the toilet paper and frowned when I touched it. It was one-ply. Few things make me as distraught as encountering one-ply tissue paper in a dude's bathroom. Not to be too dramatic, but that flimsy toilet paper makes me reconsider all of my life's choices. I work myself into a tizzy as my mind races to answer the question, *What missteps have I made that have led me to use this inferior ply?*

What if I had run for school president in high school? Do high school presidents wipe with one-ply? I don't think so! I should've worked harder in that statistics class in my junior year of college. It would've raised my GPA and—who knows?—maybe I would've snagged a better job. What if I'd gone for my MBA? Do MBA grads use one-ply? Hell no!

If I *had* gone for my MBA, I'd probably be dating a real man who had hobbies like rock climbing or windsurfing. He'd be cultured; he'd probably enjoy sipping loose teas from exotic locales. And I'll bet you ten bucks that he'd have a super-sized roll of Cottonelle (with aloe!) in his bathroom. Or maybe some NASA-developed toilet paper unavailable to the mass market that's made with ten percent cashmere and five percent kitten hair. Maybe he'd even have a heated toilet seat! Who knows what kind of toilet treats I'm missing out on?

Instead, I get to date guys that live in West Philly flophouses, drink budget whiskey, and can afford only one-ply toilet paper. I'm pretty sure prisoners get higher-quality toilet paper than this. As a child, I pictured my adult self as an adult surrounded by plush TP. Where did it all go wrong? I've not only let myself down, *but I've let my inner child down, too.*

By the time I left his bathroom, I had a dead look in my eye and I was quoting Nietzsche. I climbed into his bed, cursing myself for ever leaving the comfort and warmth of my bedroom. It turns out that staying at his house was less eighties ski chateau and more *Misery.*

I woke up with the snow piled high outside the window and a groggy Jack beside me. He must've crawled into bed during the night.

"Hey," I said.

"What? Oh, hey. What time is it?"

"I don't know. Your clock says eight thirty A.M."

He groaned and hoisted himself out of bed.

"What? No cuddling?" I pouted.

"Sorry. I gotta get ready for work. Why don't you see if Suzy's up? Maybe you can spend the day with her."

"I'm sure she's still sleeping. It's pretty early. I mean, I'll text her."

"Well, you gotta figure something out because you can't stay here."

"I thought you said that we could hang out. That was the whole point of me even coming here, Jack."

"I have work to do. I told you that. Go hang with Suzy. I'll text you when I'm done. Is it cool if you scoot soon? I have things to do."

"All right. Just let me get my things together." I gathered up all of my stuff and trekked out into the snow. I couldn't even hear him shut the door behind me because the snow was coming down so heavily. Thank God Suzy answered the door when I rang her doorbell. With twelve inches on the ground, I wasn't going anywhere I couldn't walk.

"Hey, girl!"

"Anna! Come in, come in." Her house was warm, thank God.

"I was across the street at Jack's, and you're not going to believe this, but he kicked me out of his house for the day."

"Oh, that guy is the worst. Here, take a seat. I'll make some coffee."

I had a great day with Suzy, catching up and giggling, but I started to get a strange feeling that I wasn't going to hear from Jack again. Three P.M. came with no word. Then, four P.M. Then, five P.M. Six P.M. rolled around and still no word.

"Suzy, I have a weird feeling about this. He's going to blow me off. I can feel it."

"I'm sure he's just busy," she reassured me.

Finally, at seven P.M. I texted him.

Hey. What's up?

Twenty three minutes later, I got a text back:

I think I'm just gonna lay low at my house. Um, you can come over . . . if you want.

I wrote:

Well, do you want me to come over?

Another ten minutes went by before he wrote back.

It's up to you. I mean, you can. If you want.

Nothing puts a pin in my balloon faster than a guy saying this to me. It is the most noncommittal, least enthusiastic, unfriendliest, crummiest thing to hear from someone you were excited to spend time with. Of course I want to hang out! Of course I want to come over! That's why I drove all the way over here for the blizzard. All signs point to Yes-I-Want-to-Hang-Out land.

I'm not sure if this is even scientifically possible, but I swore I could hear him shrugging through the phone. It was maddening. I felt my whole body becoming hot with anger, like when Sarah Connor grabs the fence when the nuclear bomb hits in *Terminator 2*.

I wanted to punch a pillow. I wanted to slam a heavy door. This little text exchange had essentially turned me into the Hulk. Great.

Then, like a roadside bomb, he sent this:

I think it'd be best if we were just friends. I don't think that this is going to work.

I read the message out loud to Suzy and she rolled her eyes.

"He was the one who invited *me* over in the first place! So now he's dumping me? Nothing even happened between us. He passed out on the couch. I'm sorry, the *futon*."

Suzy got up and grabbed me a beer from the fridge. "Don't worry about it. You're here with me. You're out of his rathole of a house. Don't give it another thought."

"To not thinking!" I said.

"To not thinking!" she echoed, raising her beer in the air and taking a sip. "You can stay here as long as you want. Seriously, forget him."

For the third time ever, I deleted his number from my phone.

Suzy let me crash on her couch as the snow choked off the streets. Cars weren't even cars anymore, just large lumps of snow. However, I was woken up by the sound of sharp shoveling noises. I shuffled over to the window and saw Jack trying to shovel out his car from the massive amount of snow. I had to take pause.

He was wearing his bedroom slippers, no socks, pajama pants with Homer Simpson saying "I am so smart" printed on them, a ratty T-shirt, a winter coat, and . . . that's it. Picture that outfit in your mind. Things that were missing from his snow shoveling outfit: Gloves. A hat. A scarf. Socks. Hands down, he was the most ill-prepared snow shoveler I've ever seen.

Besides his outfit being insane, the way he was swiping at the snow on his windshield with the sleeve of his coat made him look like a maniac, too. He was hopping through the snow like Puck in *A Midsummer Night's Dream* because he didn't want to get snow in his slippers. I have an idea: *Don't wear slippers outside!* I mean, who wears their slippers to shovel out their car? That's crazy!

Then, I saw Jack playfully toss a snowball at a girl standing by his front door smoking a cigarette. Holy shit. He had another girl with him. She was getting the snowball fight that he had promised me. Where the hell did she come from? The city was buried under several feet of snow and he'd somehow managed to sneak a girl into his place? Is he a magician? Was she in a closet the whole time? How'd he do that? She shrieked playfully as he pelted her with snowballs. He must have a *huge* pair of snowballs to openly flaunt her in front of me like that.

I didn't know who I was angrier at: him for tangling me in this mess or myself for ignoring the obvious signs and believing he'd changed.

It was a whole 'nother day before I could even begin to shovel my car out of the snow. I was terrified of running into him while I dug my car out. But I did it. Driving back home was like coming back from war. I was tired and drained, and I saw things no person should ever see. I made sure to put extra marshmallows in my cocoa.

I ran into Jack at a party recently and he came up to me straightaway. *Must resist his charms.* He fist-bumped me and said, "What's up, player?" which almost made me laugh.

"Hello, Jack." I did my best to project a steely façade.

"What? You're still mad at me? *Come on!* Don't be mad.

How can you be mad at a guy who dances like *this*?" Then he grabbed his friend Mark's hips and humped him from behind, causing the poor guy to spill his beer everywhere. I covered my mouth so he wouldn't see me crack up.

"There it is! I knew I could get you to smile." I tried not to grin, but it was impossible. How could I be angry at such an immature goofball? It's like getting mad that Nickelback still has a career or that a Katherine Heigl movie lacks sufficient character development. What's the point? It's the nature of the beast.

Besides, I don't enjoy being irritated at him. It's truly not worth it. Fuck it. It's easier to accept him for the wacky jerk he is. I looked at his huge hands and huge feet and realized that I wouldn't want to date him anyway. I like my men like my marshmallows: mini-sized.

Being with Jack made me feel like the mature one. Maybe I wasn't so bad at being an adult. Knowing who you are and what you want is a mature thing. I may not be ready to settle down, but at least I wasn't settling for something that wasn't a good fit. I could recognize Jack for what he was: a knucklehead. I wasn't mad at him anymore. Any anger I had for him evaporated instantly.

"You're right. I can't be angry at a guy who dances like that."

Then I scanned the place for the shortest guy in the room because, let's face it, that's my favorite thing to do.

# CHAPTER 14

# Those Who Can't, Teach

No adult woman ever wants to move back home with her parents. It's essentially waving the white flag: *Hey, everyone, I couldn't hack it in the real world.* For me, it wasn't an easy decision. And it's not like I didn't try to keep my apartment in the city. But, as it turned out, I was totally incapable of being hired for any kind of job anywhere in Philadelphia, and apparently, slices of pizza and cases of beer don't pay for themselves.

I thought graduating from grad school would be like falling back into a pile of job offers. It wasn't like that at all. I don't know if I had a sign taped to my back saying that I would make a terrible employee or what, but I went on dozens of job interviews, and I could not get hired for the life of me. I wrote thank-you notes. I wore panty hose. I shook hands with confidence. I even came close to getting a job a few times, but they went with younger, less qualified candidates. Other people seemed to get jobs all the time, but I was like job Kryptonite. I'd watch hordes of people mindlessly commute home from their jobs every evening and wonder what they had to offer that I didn't.

It turned out that having a graduate degree in journalism was not an asset; I was overqualified for every position I applied for. It was almost cliché. I approached my professors asking for advice, but they didn't have any for me. I chose to be an expert in a dying field. I might as well have gotten my master's in Betamax videotapes or Sony Walkman repair.

And it's not like I had lost a job and had unemployment benefits to bridge the gap. I was living off my savings, which were dwindling rapidly.

My friends empathized because most of them were struggling to find jobs, too. My parents just seemed perplexed by the whole thing. I'd never had any trouble nailing down jobs when I lived in New York City. But to Philly, I was doused head to toe in job repellent. I tried to console myself that it was the economy's fault, but some people had jobs. I know it's true because I'd run into them as I was on my way to interview for one. Something was up.

On the plus side, being chronically unemployed gave me a lot of free time, which allowed me to write as much as I wanted. Yay, I guess. But no one's ever put food on his or her table by writing (that statement is totally not true now that I think about it). Let me rephrase: I was not putting food on my table through writing. I had to reassess some major life goals.

As my savings grew smaller and my options became more limited, it was clear that my life was going in one direction and it wasn't to a human resources department to talk about medical benefits and the company sick day policy; it was going to a bedroom on the second floor of my parents' house. I had to accept reality here.

Another factor that influenced my decision to move home was that since Kat had moved out of the apartment we shared, my home life straight up sucked. I had a steady stream of Craigslist freakazoid roommates file in and out of her empty room. One quiet poet moved in his funky half-Asian girlfriend after three months. When I told him that I didn't appreciate the extra roommate, he abruptly moved out with her, leaving me back at square one looking for someone to split the rent.

The next roommate was an art school guy who didn't even have a bed, just a gnarly sleeping bag he'd wiggle into every night. It was weird. Besides the fact that his room smelled like a sweaty gym sock, he was hard of hearing, which made communication tricky.

Me: "Did you call the landlord back? He wanted to talk to you."

Him: "What?"

Me: "Are you planning on staying in tonight? I'm going to have some friends over."

Him: "What?"

His name was Arnie and he had just moved to Philly. I felt sorry for him, but I felt sorrier for myself because he kept trying to get in on my plans. He'd lean up against the wall looking bored every Friday afternoon and say, "So, what's going on this weekend?"

"I don't know. I was thinking about checking out the scene at Silk City."

"Oh, cool. Mind if I join you?" What do you say to that? It's hard rejecting a dude every single week. After two months he finally stopped asking, thank God.

The first time he asked, I said sure he could come out with me, because I was a nice person and I wanted to give him a shot. He had just moved his things into my place, and he didn't have a circle of friends yet. However, my pity quickly turned to irritation because he ended up getting trashed, hitting on my friend Lana relentlessly, and then asking me if he could borrow ten bucks. It was like getting mugged by a slow, horny, drunk robber who had keys to my place. I wasn't his ATM or his pimp and I didn't appreciate him creeping on my buds.

It didn't take long for our roommate relationship to go downhill. He insisted on smoking in the apartment even though it was against the lease. I had him kicked out for the offense. It was clear that this living-with-random-strangers thing wasn't working.

The roommate after that wanted to be my best friend when I just wanted to have someone to split the gas bill with. She'd talk my ear off into all hours of the night, divulging her deepest relationship problems to me. Instead of having a roommate, I had gained a psychiatric patient. I wasn't getting paid for that service, either.

I found myself heading to my parents' house for peace of mind so often that it didn't seem like that big a leap to just move home altogether. With no real job and a string of crummy roommates, it was nice to give the finger to the whole thing and retreat to the suburbs. And, as a bonus, the break from rent and bills was admittedly welcome.

At first it wasn't so bad living with my parents. It was nice having a bigger kitchen to cook elaborate meals in. It was even nicer to have other people eat the food I wanted to cook. My sister Rachel bought me a fancy apron, which was fun to wear as I breaded chicken cutlets and chopped mushrooms. The apron distracted me from the fact that it wasn't my kitchen I was cooking in.

My parents installed cable TV in my bedroom, which fucking ruled. After watching three stations back at my apartment on rabbit-ear antennae for six years, it felt like I had won the entertainment lottery to have so many cable channels on demand. And I could write all I wanted since I didn't have any annoying roommates poking their heads in, demanding that I listen to their long list of grievances. It wasn't that bad. It was almost too comfortable.

The only downside to living at my parents' was telling guys I met about my situation because it made me seem like a loser, which I sorta was. I was a hypocrite, too. After looking down on guys who'd moved home and couldn't hold a job for years, I was on the other side of the fence with my tail between my legs. I hated that part.

After a few months, my parents sat me down and insisted that I do something—anything—to get my life back on track, so I took a job substitute teaching a few days a week. Since my mom works in the school district as a learning consultant, I entered into the system quickly. My new job gave me just enough money to buy beer. Plus, I liked the flexible hours and I enjoyed interacting with the youth of America. I could accept only the jobs I wanted to take and decline ones that were either inconvenient or just didn't look fun.

But I had never been an authority figure before, and it took a while for me to fully grasp that shift. When students asked if they could go to the bathroom, I'd be like, "Why are you asking me? I don't care. Do what you gotta do." They'd exchange worried looks with their classmates. *Is this lady for real?* I treated them like adults, which blew their minds.

"Can I eat my snack now?" a little girl with pigtails would ask.

"Go for it."

"Can I write the answer on the chalkboard?" a little boy in overalls would ask.

"Knock yourself out, chief."

I became the "cool" substitute teacher, a role I enjoyed immensely. When I'd walk into the classroom, the kids would cheer and high-five each other. "We've got the cool sub," they'd exclaim. You could hear their shouts all down the hallway. Other teachers would shut their doors and give me dirty looks, trying to block out the racket. The kids would run laps around the classroom like their socks were on fire. I'm not going to deny that the ego boost was nice, especially since I was feeling pretty useless in every other area of my life.

"All right, all right. Settle down, everyone. Let's start this party." Sometimes during recess, a few of the younger kids would ask if they could hug me. If no one else was around, I'd say that they could, real fast. I felt like a rock star.

After a few weeks of subbing in the same classes, I got to know the students better. I took great pride in memorizing their names; it showed that I cared. Plus, it was easier to yell out their names when they did something out of line. And it became clear that they didn't need an apathetic woman standing in the front of the room getting chalk on her purple dress; they needed someone to maintain order, someone they could trust to take charge. I was that woman.

Not everyone liked how tough I was. Some of the students would get on my nerves, challenging my authority.

"Hey! There's no talking when I'm talking," I'd snap. "That's disrespectful."

"So?" If you've ever met a defiant seventh grader, you can imagine how this kid looked; his slouchy posture, his hair in his eyes, his muddy sneakers, and his bad attitude seemed almost calculated.

That's when the lightbulb went off: I was the authority figure in here and I had to step it up. It was my *Dangerous Minds* moment, if you will. Just so we're clear, I'm Michelle Pfeiffer in this scenario, not Coolio.

And, I have to admit, taking control of the classroom was kind of fun. I stood straighter. My voice was more commanding. I'd say things like, "In my classroom, we don't use language like that." Or, "In my classroom, we don't throw things at substitute teachers." I was concerned and fair, but if any one of those little rascals got sassy, I'd kick him the hell out. Even though I felt like a dropout in both my personal and my professional life, in the classroom I had to present myself as a confident adult.

I grew into the role and tried to be the best teacher these kids had ever had, encouraging discussions and recognizing innovations from my students. I was getting the hang of it. I subbed for four separate school districts, and I took almost every job at first because I didn't know any better. I taught everyone from kindergarteners to seniors in high school.

Things I learned after a few weeks: The younger the kids, the more psychotic they'd be about maintaining their daily routines. The older the kids, the less they cared about behaving for me. Fourth grade emerged as my favorite class to teach because these kids were still interested in behaving, yet they appreciated having a sub come in and shake things up for the day. They were my little homies.

I ate my lunch in the teachers' lounge, which was a total mindfuck. Dented Lean Cuisine boxes, sad little napkins swiped from the cafeteria, streaky plastic tablecloths; it was like having a backstage pass to the most depressing concert you've ever seen. I kept to myself and offered the other teachers only tight smiles. I wasn't interested in making friends; I was interested in teaching the kids the best I could, making my money, and going home for a nap.

At thirty-three, I was easily the youngest member on the staff. I was probably the only adult in the building that knew how to send a text message properly. Working in an office, you'd only get a half hour for lunch and two short fifteen-minute breaks. Teaching, I'd get a forty-minute lunch break and up to two more free periods. It was a good gig. I had accepted the fact that I could never be a working stiff, but teaching wasn't stiff at all; I got a kick out of it.

But, as I was busy diving into my new career, I noticed that other areas of my life were sorely lacking. I *really* missed dating guys. I wasn't meeting anyone in the suburbs. Besides, I felt like I didn't have anything to offer a guy anyway. I was too ashamed about moving home. I considered online dating again, but it seemed like too much of a hassle to explain my situation to anyone.

The only head I turned belonged to Joe, a pimply cashier at the supermarket. He had braces and a studded leather belt. Whenever I needed a quick pick-me-up, I'd make my mom go with me to his store. I'd subtly redirect her to use his aisle if he was working the register. I enjoyed making chitchat with him as my mom paid for the groceries. One day he worked up enough courage to ask me what high school I attended. My mother laughed in his face.

"Her?" She pointed at me. "She's thirty-three. She's been out of high school for a very long time." He looked surprised. My mom kept going. "In fact, she just finished grad school. You thought she was in high school? That's a good one." She even held her sides as she laughed, to drive home the point of how hilarious the notion was.

I didn't say anything. I didn't even make eye contact with Joe. We just collected our grocery bags and left. As soon as we stepped foot in the parking lot, I snapped, "*Mom!* You totally blew up my spot back there."

"Oh, honey, relax. Like you had a chance with him. He's practically a baby."

"Well, now I'll never know. We had a connection. Sort of. The way he looks into my eyes as he rings up those SnackWell's cookies—you can't fake that."

"Oh, Anna, you wouldn't want to date him anyway. He's not even twenty-one. He can't even go to a bar legally."

I frowned. "I know, but it's just nice to be noticed by the opposite sex."

"Sweetie, you'll get back on your feet soon," she said, loading the groceries in the car. "This is all temporary."

"I just thought I'd have my shit together by now, you know? I never thought I'd be the kind of person living back home in her thirties getting her kicks by chatting up the kid at the Acme."

"You're"—she struggled to find the right word—"a late bloomer. You always have been. It's just taking you a little bit longer to figure things out, that's all."

"Thanks for the pep talk, Mom. And thanks for letting me stay with you and Dad while I sort my life out."

"Like I always say, we love having you here."

With that, I reached over and hugged her. We hugged for a while, right there in the parking lot. I started to pull away, but she didn't let go. I let my shoulders relax and she lightly rubbed my back.

"Just stop flirting with teenagers, honey. The boy has braces, for crying out loud."

# ACKNOWLEDGMENTS

Denise Silvestro and everyone at Berkley Books, thank you for letting a 6'1", thirty-three-year-old, unemployed Jewish woman write a book her parents can show off to their friends. My excellent management team, Alexis Rosenzweig and Richard Nichols, thank you for believing in me.

Sarah, Mike, Julianna, Rachel, and Alex: I'm especially grateful for your support and encouragement. Grandma from the Train, Grandma from the White House, and Grandpop, I will never forget your unconditional love.

Jenna Davis, Lara Crock, Tracy Keats Wilson, and all my wonderful friends, thank you for inspiring me.

And thank you to my first crush, Michael J. Fox, whose poster has been tacked up on my bedroom wall for more than twenty-five years.